Steck-Vaughn

BOOK 2

WORLD HISTORY
and YOU

Vivian Bernstein

Consultant

Karen Tindel Wiggins
Director of Social Studies
Richardson Independent School District
Richardson, Texas

STECK-VAUGHN
COMPANY
ELEMENTARY • SECONDARY • ADULT • LIBRARY

ABOUT THE AUTHOR

Vivian Bernstein is the author of *America's Story, America's History: Land of Liberty, World Geography and You, American Government*, and *Decisions for Health*. She received her Master of Arts degree from New York University. Bernstein is active with professional organizations in social studies, education, and reading. She gives presentations to school faculties and professional groups about content area reading. Bernstein was a teacher in the New York City Public School System for a number of years.

ACKNOWLEDGMENTS

Executive Editor: Diane Sharpe
Senior Editor: Martin S. Saiewitz
Project Editor: Meredith Edgley

Design Manager: Rusty Kaim
Photo Editor: Margie Foster
Electronic Production: JoAnn Estrada

CREDITS

Cover Photography: (plane) © Clyde H. Smith/Peter Arnold, Inc., (Berlin Wall) © D. Aubert/Sygma, (train, map) © Superstock

pp.3, 4 The Granger Collection; p.5 (top) The Granger Collection, (bottom) © Grant Heilman/Grant Heilman Photography; p.6 (top) North Wind Picture Archive, (middle) Corbis/Bettmann, (bottom) The Granger Collection; p.7 (top) © Spring Industries Inc., Fort Mill, SC, (middle) © Alan Pitcairn/Grant Heilman Photography, (bottom) North Wind Picture Archive; pp.8 (all), 11 The Granger Collection; p.12 (top right) North Wind Picture Archive, (top left, bottom) The Granger Collection, (middle) Mary Evans Picture Archive; p.13 (top, middle) The Granger Collection, (bottom) Culver Pictures; p.14 (top) The Granger Collection, (bottom) Mary Evans Picture Library; p.15 (top) Mary Evans Picture Library, (bottom) Archive Photos; p.19 Corbis/Bettmann; p.20 (both) The Granger Collection; p.21 (top, middle) The Granger Collection, (bottom) Culver Pictures; p.22 (top) The Granger Collection, (bottom) © Patrick Piel/Gamma-Liaison; p.27 Corbis/Bettmann; p.28 The Granger Collection; p.29 Art Resource/Giraudon; p.30 (top) Hulton Deutsch, (bottom) The Granger Collection; pp.31, 34 The Granger Collection; p.35 Culver Pictures; p.36 (top, middle) The Granger Collection, (bottom) © Superstock; p.37 The Granger Collection; p.38 (top) National Portrait Gallery, Smithsonian Institution/Art Resource, (bottom) The Granger Collection; p.42 The Granger Collection; p.43 (top, middle) The Granger Collection, (bottom) Hulton Deutsch; p.44 The Granger Collection; p.45 (top) Corbis/Bettmann, (middle) Hulton Deutsch, (bottom) Culver Pictures; p.46 (top, bottom) Corbis/Bettmann, (middle) The Granger Collection; p.47 Culver Pictures; p.48 (top) The Granger Collection, (bottom) Hulton Deutsch; p.52 The Granger Collection; p.53 (both) Culver Pictures; p.54 Corbis/Bettmann; p.55 The Granger Collection; p.56 (top) Corbis/Bettmann, (middle) Culver Pictures; p.57 The Granger Collection; p.61 Culver Pictures; p.62 (top, middle) The Granger Collection, (bottom) Corbis/Bettmann; p.63 (top) Corbis/Bettmann, (middle) Culver Pictures, (bottom) AP/Wide World; p.64 (top) Culver Pictures, (bottom) The Granger Collection; p.65 (top) Hulton Deutsch, (bottom) Archive Photos; p.69 The Granger Collection; p.70 Archive Photos; p.71 (top, bottom) Hulton Deutsch, (middle) National Portrait Gallery, Smithsonian Institution/Art Resource; p.72 SEF/Art Resource; p.73 (top) The Granger Collection, (middle) AP/Wide World; p.76 Hulton Deutsch; p.77 Corbis/Bettmann; p.78 (top) Hulton Deutsch, (middle) Corbis/Bettmann, (bottom) National Portrait Gallery, Smithsonian Institution/Art Resource; p.79 (top, bottom) Corbis/Bettmann, (middle) AP/Wide World; p.80 AP/Wide World; p.81 (top) The Granger Collection, (bottom) AP/Wide World; p.85 © Carl Dekeyzer/Magnum Photos; p.86 (top) © Superstock, (bottom) © Les Stone/Sygma; p.87 (top) © Paul Lowe/Magnum Photos, (middle, bottom) Corbis/Bettmann; pp.90, 91 Corbis/Bettmann; p.92 (top) NASA, (bottom) Hulton Deutsch; p.93 (middle) National Portrait Gallery, Smithsonian Institution, (bottom) U.S. Airforce Photo; p.97 Corbis/Bettmann, (top, middle) Corbis/Bettmann, (bottom) AP/Wide World; p.99 Corbis/Bettmann; p.100 (top) © Stuart Franklin/Magnum Photos, (middle) © Gobet/Gamma-Liaison, (bottom) © David McIntyre/Black Star; p.101 (both) Corbis/Bettmann; p.104 © John Olson/Black Star; p.105 (top) © Buffon-Darquenne/Sygma, (bottom) © Charles Bonnay/Black Star; p.106 (top) Corbis/Bettmann, (middle) Archive Photos, (bottom) © Costa Manos/Magnum Photos; p.107 (top) © Michael Coyne/Black Star, (middle) Archive Photos, (bottom) © Peter Stone/Black Star; p.111 © Alan Schein/The Stock Market; p.112 © Superstock; p.113 © Lincoln Potter/Gamma-Liaison; p.114 (top) AP/Wide World, (middle) © Robert Nickelsberg/Gamma-Liaison, (bottom) © Baldev/Sygma; p.115 (top) © Gamma-Liaison, (bottom) © Rory Lysaght/Gamma-Liaison; p.116 (top left) © Hashimoto/Sygma, (top right, bottom) © Superstock, (middle) © Charles Gupton/The Stock Market; p.120 © Stephane Compoint/Sygma; p.121 © Kalari/Sygma; p.122 (top) © Stephane Compoint/Sygma, (middle) © Sipa Press, (bottom) © Viennareport/Sygma; p.123 Archive Photos; p.124 (top) © Maher Attar/Sygma, (bottom) © B. Markel/Gamma-Liaison; p.125 (top) AP/Wide World, (middle) © Allan Tannebaum/Sygma, (bottom) © Zohrab/Sygma; p.128 © Scott Daniel Peterson/Gamma-Liaison; p.129 © Renee Lynn/Photo Researchers; p.130 (top) © Reza/Sygma, (middle) © Renee Lynn/Photo Researchers, (bottom) © Olivier Thibaud/Sipa Press; p.131 (top) © A. Facelly/Sipa Press, (middle) © J. Polleross/The Stock Market, (bottom) © Brooks Kraft/Sygma; p.132 (top) © William Campbell/Sygma, (middle, bottom) © Superstock; p.133 (top) Reuters/Bettmann/Corbis, (bottom) © South Light/Gamma-Liaison; p.136 © Victor Englebert/Photo Researchers; p.137 © Porterfield/Chickering/Photo Researchers; p.138 (top) © Superstock, (middle) © Carl Frank/Photo Researchers, (bottom) © Anthony Suau/Gamma-Liaison; p.139 (top) © M. Wendler/Okapia/Photo Researchers, (middle) © Anthony Suau/Gamma-Liaison, (bottom) © William Campbell/Sygma; p.140 (top) Dusko Despotovic/Sygma, (middle) © Les Stone/Sygma, (bottom) © David Ball/The Stock Market; p.141 (top) © Duhab/Sipa Press, (middle) © Jimmy Rudnick/The Stock Market, (bottom) © Superstock; p.145 © Superstock; p.146 UPI/Bettmann/Corbis; p.147 (top) Reuters/Wolfgang Rattay/Archive Photos, (bottom) © Rosenfeld Images/The Stock Market; p.148 (top) Reuters/Chris Helgren/Archive Photos, (middle) © Nicholas Fievez/Sipa Press, (bottom) © Herve Donnezan/Photo Researchers; p.149 (top) © Wesolowski/Sygma, (bottom) © Sygma; p.153 NASA; p.154 © Peter Garfield/The Stock Market; p.155 (top) © Grant Heilman/Grant Heilman Photography, (middle) © Ben Simmons/The Stock Market, (bottom) © Aaron Haupt/The Stock Market; p.156 (top) © Superstock, (bottom) © Grant Heilman/Grant Heilman Photography; p.157 (top) NASA, (bottom) Science Photo Library/Photo Researchers; p.158 (top) © Pete Saloutos/The Stock Market, (middle, bottom) © Superstock; p.161 © Paul Steel/The Stock Market; p.162 (top) © Vivian Moos/The Stock Market, (bottom) © Sergio Dorantes/Sygma; p.163 (top) © Larry Downing/Sygma, (middle) Shell Offshore, Inc., (bottom) © Richard R. Hanson/Photo Researchers; p.164 (top) © Superstock, (middle) © Sygma, (bottom) © M. Denora/Gamma-Liaison; p.165 (top) © Ralph Gaillarde/Gamma-Liaison, (middle) © Regis Bossu/Sygma, (bottom) © Leonide Principe/Photo Researchers; p.168 AP/Wide World; p.169 (top) © Larry Downing/Sygma, (bottom) © Russell D. Curtis/Photo Researchers; p.170 (top) Goeff Dowen/Gamma-Liaison, (middle) © J. L. Atlan/Sygma, (bottom) © Russell D. Curtis/Photo Researchers; p.171 (top) © Patrick Forden/Sygma, (middle) © Dave Weintraub/Photo Researchers, (bottom) © Ted Horowitz/The Stock Market; p.172 (top) © Anat Givon/Sygma, (bottom) © Stuart Isett/Sygma.

ISBN 0-8172-6326-8

6 7 8 9 PO 03 02 01 00

Contents

1950

1945 World War II

1945–1991 Cold War

People in History

List of Maps

List of Skill Builders

Charts, Graphs, and Diagrams

To the Reader

You are about to read an exciting story about the world. *World History and You* tells about important changes in the world. It tells how men and women fought wars in order to win freedom. They wanted the freedom to speak as they wished, to pray as they wished, and to make laws that were fair to all. Some nations fought wars in order to become independent. At other times, nations fought wars in order to conquer and to rule other nations. World history is more than a story about wars. It is the story of how people have worked to spread peace and freedom. It is also the story of new inventions and powerful ideas that have changed the world.

World History and You will help you become a better social studies student. Start by learning the vocabulary words for each chapter. Try to review vocabulary words from earlier chapters. Study each map and think about the ways geography can change the history of a place. Then read the text of each chapter carefully. By reading the chapter a second time, you will improve your understanding of history. Complete the chapter activities carefully, and your skills in writing and social studies will improve.

As you study world history, you will learn about the ways that revolutions have changed the world. You will find out how some nations are working to avoid war and to spread peace. You will learn about mistakes people made in the past. By learning from past mistakes, you can build a better future. As you read about the past, remember that you are reading a story that will never end. As you approach the year 2000, remember that you, too, are part of the story.

Vivian Bernstein

Unit 1   A Changing World

The years between 1700 and 1900 were years of great change in the world. During this time there were many revolutions. Some revolutions were wars for independence. But other revolutions were not wars. The agricultural revolution of the 1700s was a change in the way farmers grew food. New machines were invented that helped farmers grow much more food. Fewer people were hungry.

During this time there was another kind of revolution. This revolution was a change in the way goods were made. The Industrial Revolution caused great changes in the ways people lived and worked. Many kinds of new machines were made. The new machines made work faster and easier. Many people were needed to run these new machines. People began to work in factories in cities. More and more people moved to cities. Cities grew larger.

The factories had many new problems. They were not always safe places to work. People had to work long, hard hours. As time passed, workers found ways to solve their problems. They worked together to get better pay, better hours, and safer factories.

ATLANTIC OCEAN

PACIFIC OCEAN

PACIFIC OCEAN

INDIAN OCEAN

What new machines were made in the years between 1700 and 1900? What changes did they bring? How did workers solve their problems? As you read Unit 1, think about some of the ways that the world changed between 1700 and 1900. Think about how the inventions and the changes of the Industrial Revolution affect our lives today.

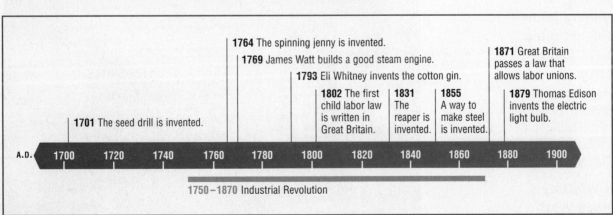

1764 The spinning jenny is invented.

1769 James Watt builds a good steam engine.

1793 Eli Whitney invents the cotton gin.

1802 The first child labor law is written in Great Britain.

1831 The reaper is invented.

1855 A way to make steel is invented.

1871 Great Britain passes a law that allows labor unions.

1879 Thomas Edison invents the electric light bulb.

1701 The seed drill is invented.

A.D. | 1700 | 1720 | 1740 | 1760 | 1780 | 1800 | 1820 | 1840 | 1860 | 1880 | 1900

1750–1870 Industrial Revolution

The Industrial Revolution

NEW WORDS

♦ Industrial Revolution
♦ seed drill
♦ factories
♦ industry
♦ spinning wheels
♦ spinning jenny
♦ spinning mule
♦ power loom
♦ cotton gin
♦ steam engine
♦ reaper

PEOPLE & PLACES

♦ Eli Whitney
♦ James Watt

Have you ever thought about how your clothes are made? Who sewed the clothes? Who made the cloth? Most people today buy clothes that were made by machines. However, just 250 years ago, most people had to make their clothes by hand. Then about the year 1750, people began to invent new machines to help them make clothes. These new machines could do work that people had always done by hand. This change is known as the **Industrial Revolution**. The Industrial Revolution was not a war. It was a change in the way goods were made.

The Industrial Revolution began with another revolution. This revolution was an agricultural revolution. The agricultural revolution was a change in the way farmers grew food. You have learned about the agricultural revolution that happened thousands of years ago during the Stone Age. Stone

During the Industrial Revolution, people began to use machines in factories. Here workers are using power looms to weave cloth.

Age people learned to plant seeds to grow food. They no longer had to move from place to place to hunt animals. The first agricultural revolution changed the way of life for Stone Age people.

For thousands of years, farmers had done most work by hand. They had planted seeds by throwing them on top of the ground. The wind blew away most of the seeds. So most of the seeds never grew. It was hard for farmers to grow enough food.

Then in 1701 the **seed drill** was invented in Great Britain. The seed drill was a machine that pushed the seeds into the soil. More seeds grew into plants. The seed drill helped farmers grow much more food. The invention of the seed drill led to the invention of many other farm machines. The seed drill was the beginning of the agricultural revolution of the 1700s and 1800s. Before long, there were also other changes. People started to have larger farms. They learned better ways to grow crops. They also raised better farm animals.

The agricultural revolution helped the Industrial Revolution begin in Great Britain. The revolution began in Great Britain for five main reasons. One reason was that Great Britain had a large population. There were many British people who were interested in science and inventions. There were also many people who could work in new **factories**. Because one farmer could grow more food, fewer farmers were needed. People moved to cities to work.

A second reason was that Great Britain had many natural resources. Many resources were needed to start the Industrial Revolution. Great Britain had a lot of iron, coal, rivers, and streams. Iron was needed to make machines. Coal was needed to provide power to run machines. Rivers and streams were needed to provide water power to run machines. Great Britain also had a lot of sheep for wool cloth.

A third reason the Industrial Revolution began in Great Britain was that there were no wars on British

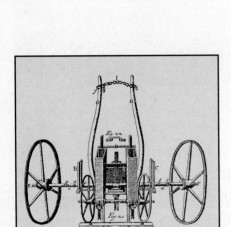

Seed drill

People used sheep's wool to make cloth.

The first factories of the Industrial Revolution were built near water.

Woman using a spinning wheel

Spinning jenny

land. Years of peace in Great Britain gave people more time and money to invent new machines.

A fourth reason the Industrial Revolution began in Great Britain was that Great Britain had a good banking system. The banking system helped people have more money. Many people had money to buy goods. Rich merchants used their money to buy machines and build factories. They also bought ships. They used their ships to take goods to far-off places.

A fifth reason was Great Britain's good location. The British could move goods to and from many other lands easily by sea. Great Britain also has many harbors. British ships left the harbors to carry goods to other countries for trade.

The cloth **industry** was the first business to change because of the Industrial Revolution. People all over the world wanted to buy more wool and cotton cloth. Most cloth was made at home. Workers who made cloth at home could not make enough cloth. For a long time, the British had used **spinning wheels** at home to make thread. A spinning wheel could only spin one thread at a time. It took a long time to make thread on a spinning wheel at home.

About 1764 a machine called the **spinning jenny** was invented in Great Britain. This machine could

Many machines today are similar to those invented during the Industrial Revolution. These machines are weaving cloth.

Cotton

Cotton gin

spin up to eight threads at one time. A worker turned a wheel to make the jenny spin. The spinning jenny was much faster than the spinning wheel. Then in 1779 the **spinning mule** was invented. This new machine used water power to spin thread. The spinning mule was better than the jenny because it could spin much more thread more quickly.

People made cloth by weaving many threads together on a loom. For thousands of years, weaving had been done by hand. The British wanted a loom that could weave thread into cloth quickly. In 1785 a machine called the **power loom** was invented in Great Britain. The power loom used water power to weave cloth. People could now make a lot of cloth quickly. They began to need more natural resources, such as cotton. Many people used cotton to make cloth. Farmers could not grow enough cotton.

Large cotton crops were grown in the United States. Seeds had to be pulled out of the cotton plant. Then the cotton could be used to make cloth. Workers used to pick the cotton seeds out of the plant by hand. This was slow work. Then in 1793 an American named Eli Whitney invented a machine called the **cotton gin**. The cotton gin quickly pulled the seeds from the cotton. One cotton gin could do the work of fifty people. Farmers began to grow

James Watt

Watt's steam engine

A reaper

larger cotton crops. Soon the United States had more cotton to sell to Great Britain.

The Industrial Revolution changed the ways that people lived and worked. For hundreds of years, most families had worked together at home. The new spinning and weaving machines were too big to be used at home. Merchants built factories for the new machines. The factory owners hired many people to work in the factories.

At first, water power was used to run the new spinning and weaving machines. Water power made the machines work. Factories that needed water power had to be built close to rivers and streams. It was not always easy to build factories near water.

People tried to find better ways to run machines so that factories could be built away from rivers and streams. People learned that they could burn coal to make hot water for steam power. In 1769 James Watt built a good **steam engine** in Great Britain. By 1800 this steam engine was being used to run machines in factories. Factories could be run by steam power instead of by water power. A steam engine could be used anywhere. Factories did not have to be built near streams or rivers.

People continued to invent other machines. For thousands of years, wheat has been used to make bread. Before the Industrial Revolution, farmers had cut wheat by hand. In 1831 an American invented the **reaper**. This new machine cut wheat quickly. Farmers began to grow a lot more wheat. People soon had more bread to eat.

As time passed, more and more people left farms to work in factories. Many factories were in cities. More people moved to the cities to find jobs in factories. Cities grew larger. As you read the next chapter, you will learn more about the Industrial Revolution. You will learn more about how it changed the ways people lived and worked.

Using Vocabulary

Finish the Paragraph Use the words in dark print to finish the paragraph below. Write on the correct blank lines the words you choose.

spinning mule   **power loom**   **Industrial**
factories   **spinning jenny**

The _____ Revolution was a change from making goods by hand to making goods by machine. Some of the first new machines were made for the cloth industry. The _____ was the first machine that could spin several threads at the same time. The _____ was a machine that used water power to spin thread. The _____ used water power to weave threads into cloth. These machines were very big. People began to use the machines in places called _____ .

Read and Remember

Find the Answer Put a check (✔) next to each sentence that tells why the Industrial Revolution began in Great Britain. You should check four sentences.

_____ **1.** Great Britain had a large population.

_____ **2.** Great Britain had a lot of natural resources, such as iron and coal.

_____ **3.** Great Britain had a very rainy climate.

_____ **4.** Great Britain had a good banking system.

_____ **5.** Great Britain was the largest island in Europe.

_____ **6.** There were no wars on British land.

Journal Writing

Write a few sentences about an invention from this chapter that you feel was the most important invention during the Industrial Revolution.

Crossword Puzzle

Each sentence below has a word missing. Choose the missing word for each sentence from the words in dark print. Then write the words in the correct places on the puzzle.

─────────────────── **ACROSS** ───────────────────

steam   Whitney   agricultural   coal

1. The Industrial Revolution actually began with an _____ revolution.

2. The cotton gin was invented by an American named Eli _____ .

3. One of Great Britain's most important natural resources was _____ .

4. In 1769 James Watt invented a good _____ engine that provided power for machines in factories.

─────────────────── **DOWN** ───────────────────

industry   drill   reaper   harbors

5. Great Britain shipped goods from its many _____ to other countries.

6. The seed _____ led to the invention of many other farm machines.

7. The cloth _____ was the first business to change because of the Industrial Revolution.

8. The _____ was invented in 1831 to help farmers cut wheat quickly.

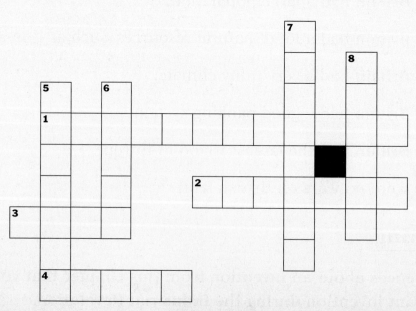

The Industrial Revolution Brings Change

THINK ABOUT AS YOU READ

1. How did the Industrial Revolution change the way people traveled?
2. What other changes did the Industrial Revolution bring?
3. What were some of the problems caused by the Industrial Revolution?

NEW WORDS

♦ steam locomotive
♦ steamboat
♦ canals
♦ vaccine
♦ smallpox
♦ bacteria
♦ working class
♦ standard of living
♦ elements
♦ radiation

PEOPLE & PLACES

♦ Suez Canal
♦ Red Sea
♦ Elijah McCoy
♦ Thomas Edison
♦ Louis Pasteur
♦ Marie Curie
♦ Pierre Curie

The Industrial Revolution began in Great Britain. The new inventions helped many British people earn more money. At first, the British tried to keep their inventions a secret. But they could not stop the Industrial Revolution from spreading to other parts of the world. Soon it spread to the rest of Europe and to the United States. Later, it spread to other parts of the world. The Industrial Revolution changed the ways people all over the world lived and worked. Some changes made life better. Other changes caused problems.

The Industrial Revolution gave people better ways to travel. Before the revolution, people had traveled on horses or by ships. Then in 1804 the first **steam locomotive** was built in Great Britain. The steam locomotive was a train car with a steam engine. The

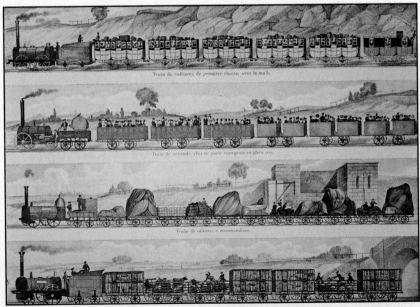

The steam locomotive changed the ways that people traveled and sent goods on land.

The first train in Japan

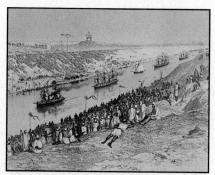
The Suez Canal in 1869

A steel factory

The steamboat was a fast way to travel because it did not need wind to move.

locomotive was strong enough to pull other train cars. The trains traveled on rails. Steam locomotives moved faster than horses. Soon many people traveled in trains pulled by locomotives. It cost less money to send goods on trains than on carts pulled by horses. The railroads also helped other industries grow.

People also wanted to travel in faster ships. For hundreds of years, people had traveled in ships with sails. The wind blew these ships across the sea. Then in 1807 a good **steamboat** was built. The steamboat had a steam engine that moved the ship. People no longer had to wait for wind to move their ships.

As people invented better ways to travel, they began to find other ways to help them travel more quickly. They began to build better roads. They also built **canals**. Canals are water routes that connect rivers, lakes, and oceans. The canals cross land to connect these bodies of water. By using the canals, merchants no longer had to move their goods from a ship, then across land, and then to another ship. One important canal is the Suez Canal, which was built in 1869. This canal connects the Mediterranean Sea with the Red Sea near Egypt. Better roads and new canals helped people save time and money.

Strong metal was needed to build machines, factories, and railroads. Great Britain had a lot of iron. For a while, iron was used to build machines, factories, and railroads. But iron is not as strong as

Elijah McCoy

Thomas Edison

Louis Pasteur

the metals we use today. In 1855 a way to change iron into a stronger metal was invented in Great Britain. First, the iron was made very clean and very hot. Then some materials were added to the hot, clean iron to change it into steel. Steel is a very strong metal. Steel railroads last longer than iron railroads. People began to use steel to build new machines and steam locomotives.

People found other ways to improve their machines and factories. In the 1870s an African American named Elijah McCoy invented a way to help trains and other machines run better. In the past, people had to stop their machines to oil them. Businesses lost a lot of time and money while the machines were turned off. McCoy invented a better way for people to oil machines without having to turn them off.

Other inventions of the Industrial Revolution made life easier. One of these was the electric light bulb. For hundreds of years, people had used candles to light their homes. In 1879 an American named Thomas Edison invented the electric light bulb. Soon electric light bulbs were being used in homes and in factories. Electricity would become a very important part of other inventions.

There were many other advances in science during the revolution. New discoveries in medicine helped people stay healthy. In 1796 a **vaccine** was developed to prevent **smallpox**. Smallpox was a disease that had killed millions of people.

In the 1860s the French scientist Louis Pasteur studied tiny living things called **bacteria**. He found that bacteria caused many diseases. Pasteur also discovered that bacteria could be killed through heat. Pasteur's ideas were used to make milk safer to drink. Many of Pasteur's ideas were used to solve other problems in medicine.

During the Industrial Revolution, two groups of people became very important. These groups were the **working class** and the middle class. The people of the working class worked in mines and factories. The working class grew larger as more factories were built. The middle class included factory owners and merchants. The Industrial Revolution helped the middle class become a very large and powerful group. People in the middle class had more money than people in the working class had.

The Industrial Revolution helped improve the **standard of living**. Many people earned more money. They were able to buy the things they needed or wanted. People could travel more easily. More people had jobs. People had better food and better medicine. But the Industrial Revolution also caused new problems.

A crowded city during the Industrial Revolution

As people created more machines, factories were built very quickly. Many factories were not safe places to work. The new factories and the need for many workers made cities grow too quickly. The cities were not planned very well. Many factories and other buildings were built too close together. Cities were very crowded. Diseases and fires spread very quickly through the crowded cities.

The factories also caused pollution. The factories put a lot of smoke into the air. They also put dirty liquids into rivers and streams. There was a lot of garbage created by factories and by the large populations in the cities.

Pollution from factories

The Industrial Revolution changed the way of life for millions of people. As time passed, more and more inventions would be made. Inventions such as the telegraph, the telephone, and the automobile would soon be made. But with the changes came problems, too. Cities were crowded, and pollution increased. As you read the next chapter, you will learn that life for working-class people was hard. You will also read how working-class people worked to solve their problems.

Marie Curie (1867–1934)

The Industrial Revolution led to many changes in farming, industry, and science. People continued to make many new discoveries in the late 1800s and the early 1900s. The discoveries changed the way that scientists thought about nature. An important scientist during this time was Marie Curie.

Marie was born in Warsaw, Poland, during the Industrial Revolution. Her name was Marie Sklodowska. From a young age, Marie enjoyed math and science. After high school, Marie went to the University of Paris in France. She became a Doctor of Science in 1903.

Marie married Pierre Curie while she was at the university. Pierre Curie was a teacher and a scientist. The Curies worked together on science experiments. Together they found two new **elements**. Everything in nature is made up of different elements. The Curies discovered that one of these two elements releases a powerful energy called **radiation**. In 1903 Marie and Pierre Curie and another scientist received the Nobel Prize for their work.

In 1906 Pierre Curie died. The University of Paris asked Marie Curie to take the place of her husband as a teacher at the school. Marie Curie became the first woman teacher at the University of Paris.

Marie Curie continued to study radiation. In 1911 Curie received another Nobel Prize for her work with radiation and the two elements. The study of radiation has led to great changes in medicine. Today radiation is used to treat cancer and to make x-rays. Marie Curie's work with radiation helped make people's lives better.

Marie Curie

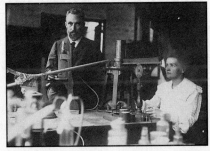
Pierre and Marie Curie at work

Questions about People in History are shown with this star on the Using What You Learned pages.

Using Vocabulary

Match Up   Finish the sentences in Group A with words from Group B. Write the letter of each correct answer on the blank line.

Group A

1. A _____ was a train that used a steam engine for its power.

2. The _____ was a large group of people who worked in mines and in factories.

3. A _____ is a water route that crosses land to connect bodies of water.

4. A _____ is medicine that prevents people from getting a disease.

5. A _____ shows how well a person is able to buy the things that he or she wants or needs.

Group B

a. canal

b. standard of living

c. vaccine

d. working class

e. steam locomotive

Read and Remember

Who Am I?   Read each sentence. Then look at the words in dark print for the name of the person who might have said it. Write on the blank after each sentence the name of the person you choose.

Marie Curie   Thomas Edison   Elijah McCoy   Louis Pasteur

1. "I invented a better way for people to oil machines." _____

2. "I won two Nobel Prizes for my work in science." _____

3. "I found a way to use electricity to light homes and factories."

   _____

4. "I discovered that bacteria cause many diseases." _____

Write the Answer   Write one or more sentences to answer each question.

1. What are three things that helped people travel more quickly? _____

_____

2. How is steel made? _____

_____

3. In what ways did the Industrial Revolution help improve the standard of

living? _____

_____

4. What were some of the problems that were caused by the Industrial

Revolution? _____

_____

5. How did Marie Curie's work help modern medicine? _____

_____

Think and Apply

Categories   Read the words in each group. Decide how they are alike. Find
the best title for each group from the words in dark print. Write the title on
the line above each group. The first one is done for you.

Inventors   Middle Class   Working Class   Ways to Travel

1. _____Middle Class_____

owned factories
often had a lot of money
became powerful

2. _____

carts
steamboats
steam locomotives

3. _____

worked in mines
worked in factories
had a hard life

4. _____

Elijah McCoy
Thomas Edison
Eli Whitney

Skill Builder

Reading a Chart   A **chart** lists a group of facts. Charts help you learn facts quickly. Read the chart below about inventions made during the Industrial Revolution. Then write the answer to each question.

SOME INVENTIONS MADE DURING THE INDUSTRIAL REVOLUTION

Invention	Inventor	Year Invented	Purpose of Invention
Spinning jenny	James Hargreaves	1764	To spin many threads at one time.
Steam engine	James Watt	1769	To be a source of power to run machines.
Cotton gin	Eli Whitney	1793	To pull the seeds from cotton.
Smallpox vaccine	Edward Jenner	1796	To prevent people from dying from the smallpox disease.
Steam locomotive	Richard Trevithick	1804	To move people and goods across land.
Steamboat	Robert Fulton	1807	To move people and goods across water.
Electric light bulb	Thomas Edison	1879	To provide light for homes and factories.

1. Who invented the spinning jenny? _____

2. What was invented in 1769? _____

3. What invention could pull the seeds from cotton? _____

4. What invention did Thomas Edison make? _____

5. What two inventions were made to move people and goods? _____

_____

6. When was the smallpox vaccine invented? _____

7. What was the purpose of the steam engine? _____

_____

Workers Solve Some Problems

THINK ABOUT AS YOU READ

1. Why was life hard for the working class?

2. What kinds of changes did the working class want?

3. How do labor unions work to make changes?

NEW WORDS

♦ immigrants
♦ wages
♦ working conditions
♦ cotton mills
♦ labor unions
♦ strike

What was it like to be a factory worker in Great Britain about the year 1800? Many factories were dirty and dangerous. Many workers had to work 14 hours every day. People had to work hard, but they were paid very little money.

Life was hard for the working class during the Industrial Revolution. Parents often could not earn enough money for their families by working in factories. Children often had to work, too. Some children who were as young as six years old went to work in factories. Factory owners paid women and children less money than they paid men.

Thousands of children worked in factories. Other poor children were sent to dig for coal in coal mines. Children worked at least six days a week in factories

Many children were forced to work long hours in factories. Often the factories were dangerous places to work.

One of the first labor laws said that children were no longer allowed to be coal workers.

and coal mines. They often worked more than ten hours a day. They could not go to school. They had no time for play. The factories and the coal mines were dirty and dangerous. Factory owners often beat children if they did not like the work the children did. Children became sick from working in factories and coal mines. Many children died.

Factory workers had other problems. Sometimes there was not enough work in a factory for all the workers. Then some workers would lose their jobs. Many factory workers were hurt while doing dangerous work. If they were hurt and could not work, they lost their jobs. People without jobs did not earn money. They did not have money to buy food for their families.

Many working-class people in Europe thought that they could solve their problems by moving to the United States. They thought they would have a better life in the United States. The invention of the steamboat made it possible for millions of people to move to the United States. These **immigrants** came from Great Britain and other countries in Europe.

Immigrants from Europe

People in the working class began to demand changes.

An immigrant family arriving in the United States

Women working in a glove factory

But the Industrial Revolution also changed life in the United States. Immigrants found life in the United States hard, too.

Other working-class people tried to make changes in their own countries. The working class wanted many changes. They wanted better pay, or **wages**. They wanted to work fewer hours each day. They wanted new laws to say that women and children could not work in the mines. They also wanted better **working conditions**. This means that they wanted factories and mines to be cleaner and safer. It also means they wanted to be paid if they were hurt on the job and could not work.

Many countries wrote labor laws to help their workers. Great Britain was the first country to write such laws. This was because the first factories of the Industrial Revolution began there. Then laws to help workers were written in other countries.

How did the new laws help the workers? In 1802 the first child labor law was written in Great Britain. This law said that certain children who were less than nine years old could not work in **cotton mills**. The law also said that children could not work more than 12 hours a day. Then more labor laws were written. Women and children were not allowed to work in coal mines. Children who were less than 18 years old could not work in factories. A law in 1847 said that women and children should not work more than ten hours a day in factories. Laws were also written to make factories safer.

There were still many problems for workers in factories and in mines. Workers started **labor unions**. A labor union is a group of workers that join together to solve problems. Workers in a union are called union members. Every union has leaders.

The first unions began in Great Britain in the early 1800s. But Great Britain used laws to prevent workers from starting labor unions. In 1871 the laws were changed, and labor unions were able to help the workers. Soon unions became important in the United States and in Europe. Unions began in India and Japan in the 1890s. Labor unions soon started in countries in many parts of the world.

How do labor unions help workers solve their problems? Union members might want better wages. They might want better working conditions. The union leaders talk with the factory owners. The leaders ask the factory owners to give workers better wages or better working conditions.

Sometimes factory owners agree to make changes. But sometimes they say no. If union leaders and factory owners do not agree, then union members sometimes **strike**. A strike means that union members stop working until owners and union members agree on a way to solve a problem.

Factories cannot make goods when workers are on strike. Factory owners do not want their workers to strike. So many times factory owners will give their workers better wages and working conditions. In this way unions help their members. Labor unions have been helping their members for many years.

There are still some countries in the world today that allow children to work in factories. But most countries have laws that protect their workers. Factories are safer. Working conditions are better. Today most people have a better life because of the Industrial Revolution and the work of labor unions.

Many people were injured during this strike in 1892.

Modern labor union strike in Germany

Using Vocabulary

Finish Up   Choose the word or words in dark print that best complete each sentence. Write the word or words on the correct blank line.

immigrants   working conditions   strike
labor unions   wages

1. Workers formed _____ because they wanted to work together for better labor laws.

2. People who move to one country from another are _____.

3. Many factory workers wanted better pay, or _____.

4. A _____ is when union members stop working until owners agree to make changes.

5. Safe factories and high wages are examples of good _____.

Read and Remember

Choose the Answer   Draw a circle around the correct answer.

1. Factory owners paid women and children _____ they paid men.

   more money than   less money than   the same amount as

2. Workers wanted _____.

   longer hours   lower wages   safer factories

3. The invention of the _____ made it possible for millions of people to move from Europe to the United States.

   railroad   seed drill   steamboat

4. In 1802 the first child labor law was written for children in _____.

   schools   cotton mills   coal mines

5. In 1871 British laws were changed to allow workers to start _____.

   labor unions   their own factories   working with machines

Think and Apply

Drawing Conclusions   Read the first two sentences below. Then read the third sentence. Notice how it follows from the first two sentences. The third sentence is called a **conclusion**.

> Many factories used water power from rivers and streams. The steam engine used coal to power machines.

> **CONCLUSION**   Factories that used steam engines did not have to be built near rivers and streams.

Read each pair of sentences. Then look in the box for the conclusion you can make. Write the letter of the conclusion on the blank. The first one is done for you.

1. Parents often could not earn enough money to feed their families.
Many factory owners beat children who worked for them.

Conclusion ___b___

2. Factories in Europe had poor working conditions.
Workers thought life in the United States would be better.

Conclusion _____

3. Factory workers wanted better pay and a shorter workday.
Factory workers needed to work together to get changes made.

Conclusion _____

4. Children in Great Britain often had to work long hours in dangerous factories and mines.
Today British children are not allowed to work in factories and in mines.

Conclusion _____

> **a.** Factory workers started labor unions to help solve their problems.
> **b.** Life was hard for the working class.
> **c.** Many European workers moved to the United States.
> **d.** Great Britain passed child labor laws.

Skill Builder

Reading a Line Graph   Graphs are drawings that help you compare facts. The graph below is a **line graph**. A line graph shows how something changes over time. The line graph below shows how many people worked in British coal mines from 1831 to 1871. Study the graph. Then circle the words or dates that best complete the sentences below.

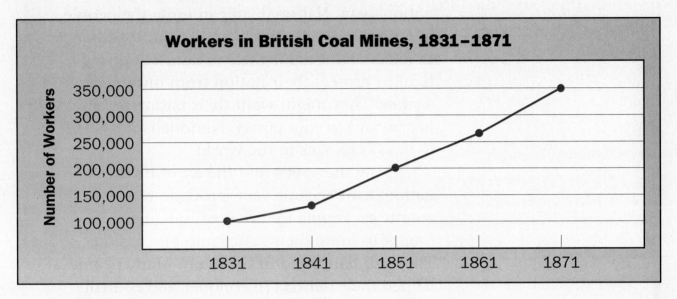

Workers in British Coal Mines, 1831–1871

1. The graph shows the number of coal miners in _____.

   the United States   Great Britain   France

2. The graph shows the number of coal miners from 1831 to _____.

   1821   1871   1881

3. The year with the fewest coal miners was _____.

   1831   1841   1861

4. There were about 200,000 coal miners in _____.

   1841   1851   1861

5. There were about 350,000 coal miners in _____.

   1851   1861   1871

6. From 1831 to 1871, the number of coal miners _____.

   grew smaller   grew larger   stayed the same

Unit 2   Nationalism, Imperialism, and War

Are you very proud of your nation? When people feel great pride for their nation, that pride is called nationalism. Nationalism can unite the people of a nation. It can help people work together to make changes for their nation. They might fight to protect their nation from invading armies. They might want their nation to grow in size and to gain power. Nationalism has led to many changes in the world.

During the 1800s and the early 1900s, nationalism became very strong in many countries. People in different Italian states fought to unite their states into one nation. This also happened in Germany. Many people helped their nations to conquer and control other lands in places like Asia and Africa. Nations built strong armies because of nationalism. Nationalism has led to terrible wars.

Other changes also occurred during this time period. The sizes of many nations changed at the end of wars. A major revolution occurred in Russia. Some nations started new kinds of governments. New dictators came to power. The Great Depression hurt nations all over the world.

How did Italy and Germany become new nations? Why did nations want to conquer other lands? How did the ideas of a few people affect millions of people in the world? As you read Unit 2, think about the good and bad effects of nationalism. Think about the conditions in the world that led to a world war and to new dictators.

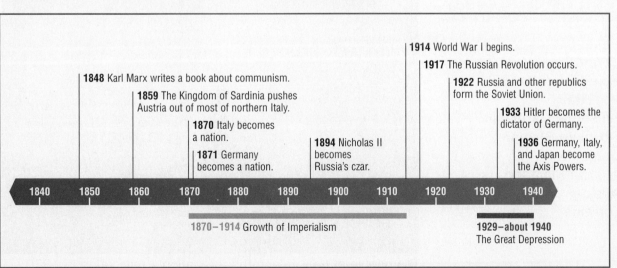

1848 Karl Marx writes a book about communism.

1859 The Kingdom of Sardinia pushes Austria out of most of northern Italy.

1870 Italy becomes a nation.

1871 Germany becomes a nation.

1894 Nicholas II becomes Russia's czar.

1914 World War I begins.

1917 The Russian Revolution occurs.

1922 Russia and other republics form the Soviet Union.

1933 Hitler becomes the dictator of Germany.

1936 Germany, Italy, and Japan become the Axis Powers.

| 1840 | 1850 | 1860 | 1870 | 1880 | 1890 | 1900 | 1910 | 1920 | 1930 | 1940 |

1870–1914 Growth of Imperialism

1929–about 1940 The Great Depression

The Unification of Germany and Italy

Italy and Germany became nations in the 1870s. Before that, Italy and Germany were divided into many independent states. Each state had its own ruler and laws. But people wanted the states to unite. They had strong feelings of **nationalism**. Nationalism means love and pride for one's nation. Nationalism helps unite people. Feelings of nationalism helped the Italian and German states to become new nations.

It was not easy for the Italian states to become one nation. After the Congress of Vienna, there were nine Italian states. Austria controlled many of the northern states of Italy. Southern Italy was ruled by a king. Between northern Italy and southern Italy were the Papal States. The Papal States belonged to the Roman Catholic Church.

A man named Count Camillo di Cavour helped unite Italy. He was the **prime minister** of the

The people of Italy celebrated the nation's unification in 1870.

ITALY BEFORE UNIFICATION

SWITZERLAND
SAVOY
FRANCE
AUSTRIA
LOMBARDY
VENETIA
Venice
KINGDOM
OF SARDINIA
TUSCANY
CORSICA
(French)
PAPAL
STATES
Rome
Adriatic Sea
Mediterranean
Sea
KINGDOM
OF THE
TWO SICILIES
AFRICA
N W E S

ITALY AFTER UNIFICATION

SWITZERLAND
FRANCE
AUSTRIA
Venice
CORSICA
(French)
ITALY
1870
SARDINIA
Rome
Adriatic Sea
Mediterranean
Sea
AFRICA
SICILY
N W E S

Many Italian states united to become the nation of Italy. Which two states included large islands?

Count Camillo di Cavour

Kingdom of Sardinia, one of the nine Italian states. Cavour hoped that all the states of Italy would unite. But he knew that first the northern states of Italy had to be freed from Austria.

Cavour asked other European nations to help the Italians fight the Austrians. France agreed to help the Kingdom of Sardinia. When Austria **declared war** on Sardinia in 1859, French and Italian soldiers went to fight. They pushed the Austrians out of most of northern Italy. By 1860 most of the northern states had joined with the Kingdom of Sardinia. Austria still ruled the northern state of Venetia.

Once the northern states had united, an Italian named Giuseppe Garibaldi sailed to southern Italy. In 1860 Garibaldi and his army captured southern Italy. Then Garibaldi and Cavour's soldiers conquered the Papal States. They did not conquer Rome because France was protecting the city. Except for Venetia and Rome, most of the Italian states were united. In 1861 these united states became known as the Kingdom of Italy.

Giuseppe Garibaldi

Pope Pius IX, the pope during Italy's unification

In 1866 Italy joined Prussia in a war against Austria. Austria lost the war. As part of the peace treaty, Austria had to give the state of Venetia to Italy. Then in 1870 France and Prussia went to war against each other. So France removed its soldiers from Rome. The Italian army then conquered Rome. The pope was allowed to rule a small part of Rome. The **unification** of Italy was complete. Italy had become one nation.

The new Italian government had problems. It needed money. Also, the pope was angry that he had lost control of Rome and of the Papal States. He told Roman Catholics not to support the new government. But Italy remained **unified**. It slowly grew stronger.

Like Italy, the 39 German states did not easily become a nation. The Congress of Vienna had joined the 39 states together to form a group called the **German Confederation**. But the 39 states had independent governments. The strongest German states were Austria and Prussia. Each of the 39 states was ruled by a prince or a king.

Otto von Bismarck led the unification of Germany. He was the prime minister of the state of Prussia. Bismarck said that wars with other countries would unite the German people. He believed that winning wars would help the growth of German nationalism.

Bismarck led the Germans in three wars. The first war was in 1864. Prussia and Austria fought together against Denmark. They won the war. They then controlled two states of Denmark.

Bismarck wanted to force Austria to leave the German Confederation. In 1866 Prussia went to war against Austria. After seven weeks, Prussia won the war. The two states from Denmark and small areas of Austria then belonged to Prussia. It was during this war that Austria lost Venetia to Italy. After the war, northern Germany was united as a new North German Confederation. Austria was no longer a German power. It became Austria-Hungary.

GERMANY BEFORE UNIFICATION

DENMARK
HANOVER
NETHERLANDS
PRUSSIA
PRUSSIA
Berlin
BAV.
SAXONY
BAVARIA
LORRAINE
AUSTRIA
ALSACE
SWITZ.
FRANCE

MAP KEY
—— German Confederation

GERMANY AFTER UNIFICATION

DENMARK
NETHERLANDS
Berlin
GERMANY
BELGIUM
LORRAINE
AUSTRIA-HUNGARY
ALSACE
SWITZ.
FRANCE
ITALY

Germany became united by 1871. Did the new nation include all of the areas that were part of the German Confederation?

Otto von Bismarck

Bismarck decided that a war against France would unite all Germans. In 1870 southern Germans helped the North German Confederation defeat the French. In 1871 the southern Germans joined the confederation and formed one nation. This new nation was called the German Empire. A new **kaiser,** or emperor, ruled the empire. The kaiser said that Bismarck would run the German government.

As a result of the war in 1870, Bismarck forced France to give most of two small French states to Germany. The two French states were Alsace and Lorraine. Alsace and Lorraine had coal and iron. Bismarck wanted this coal and iron for German factories. France was also forced to pay a lot of money to Germany. France hated Germany for many years after the war.

Bismarck worked to make the German Empire strong. He also tried to find European nations that would help protect the new nation.

Nationalism was very strong in Europe for many years. Feelings of nationalism would make nations want to rule colonies in many parts of the world. How did nations conquer and rule colonies? You will learn the answer in Chapter 5.

Using Vocabulary

Find the Meaning   Write on the blank the word or words that best complete each sentence.

1. If one nation **declares war** on another nation, then the two nations are

_____ in battle.

allies   enemies   equal

2. The **prime minister** is the _____ of a nation.

government leader   monarch   Church leader

3. The **unification** of Italy meant that Italy was _____.

one nation   several states   smaller in size

4. The **kaiser** was the German _____.

army   government   emperor

Read and Remember

Finish the Paragraph   Use the words in dark print to finish the paragraph below. Write on the correct blank lines the words you choose.

Lorraine   nationalism   states   wars   Austria

It was difficult for Germany and Italy to become nations. They each had to

unite their many _____. For Italy to become unified, the Italians

first had to free the northern states from _____. In Germany,

Otto von Bismarck said that _____ with other countries would

increase German _____. This would help unite the German

people. After a war with France, the German Empire gained most of the land of

the two states of Alsace and _____.

Think and Apply

Compare and Contrast Read each sentence below. Decide whether it tells about Germany, Italy, or both nations. Write a **G** next to each sentence that tells about Germany. Write an **I** next to each sentence that tells about Italy. Write **GI** next to each sentence that tells about both Germany and Italy. The first one is done for you.

_G_ **1.** There were 39 states that united to form this nation.

_____ **2.** Cavour and Garibaldi led the unification of this nation.

_____ **3.** The Kingdom of Sardinia pushed Austria out of the northern states to help the unification of this nation.

_____ **4.** Feelings of nationalism helped the unification of the states.

_____ **5.** This nation gained Venetia after helping Prussia defeat Austria in 1866.

_____ **6.** Wars against Denmark, Austria, and France helped unite this nation.

_____ **7.** Much of the fight for unification took place during the 1860s.

Skill Builder

Using Map Directions The four main directions are **north, south, east,** and **west**. On maps these directions are shown by a **compass rose**. The compass rose sometimes shortens the directions to **N, S, E,** and **W**. Study the map on page 29 that shows Italy before its unification. Find the compass rose. Then finish each sentence below with the word **north, south, east,** or **west**.

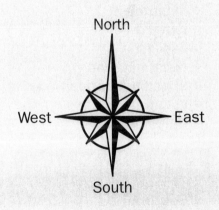

1. Austria is _____ of Switzerland.

2. Lombardy and Venetia are _____ of the Papal States.

3. The island that is part of the Kingdom of Sardinia is _____ of France.

4. Rome is _____ of the Adriatic Sea.

CHAPTER 5

Imperialism

THINK ABOUT AS YOU READ

1. **What were some of the reasons for the growth of imperialism?**
2. **Where were most of the colonies located?**
3. **How did imperialist nations gain trade rights in Japan and in China?**

NEW WORDS

♦ imperialism
♦ imperialist
♦ expand
♦ sepoys
♦ discrimination
♦ Spanish-American War
♦ opium
♦ Opium War

PEOPLE & PLACES

♦ South Africa
♦ Queen Victoria
♦ Hawaii
♦ Puerto Rico
♦ Guam
♦ Japanese

Imperialism means one nation wins control of colonies or other nations. A nation that controls colonies is called an **imperialist** nation. Imperialism occurred in ancient times. The ancient Persians and ancient Greeks were imperialists. The Roman Empire was imperialist. Between 1870 and 1914, many European and Asian nations became imperialist nations.

There were four main reasons for the growth of imperialism. One reason was that the Industrial Revolution created a need for raw materials. Many European nations needed cotton, iron, and other raw materials for their factories. They got many raw materials from countries in Africa, Asia, the Middle East, and Latin America.

Another reason for the growth of imperialism was that many merchants wanted new markets in which to sell their goods. There were millions of people in

For many years, the British controlled the land and the people of India. The British used many Indians as servants.

Imperialism in Africa

MAP KEY

Belgian	Italian
British	Portuguese
French	Spanish
German	Independent nation

British soldiers in Africa

Africa and in Asia. Imperialist nations hoped to sell many goods to these large populations.

A third reason was that many European nations felt that they had a right to conquer lands in Asia and in Africa. The Industrial Revolution had not reached many of these areas. Europeans felt that they were bringing new machines and ideas to their colonies. Colonies in Africa and Asia became good places to build factories. Many people in these colonies worked for low wages.

A fourth reason for the growth of imperialism was nationalism. Great Britain was the first nation to rule many colonies in Africa and Asia. As Great Britain's empire grew, other nations began to want new lands, too. Countries such as France, Germany, the United States, and Japan were eager to **expand** their empires. People felt proud when their nation ruled a large empire. They thought that the colonies would make their nations greater and stronger.

By 1914 most of Asia and Africa was ruled by a few nations in Europe. Look at the maps on this page and on page 37. The maps show the areas in Africa and Asia that imperialist nations ruled in 1914.

The imperialist nations often sent soldiers to capture land and to make people work for them. In Africa, Europeans used weapons to make millions of Africans work in mines and on plantations. They also forced people in the colonies to pay high taxes. Africans had to work for Europeans in order to pay these high taxes.

Great Britain ruled more land and more people than any other nation ruled. Its empire included India, Egypt, South Africa, and many other colonies. By controlling South Africa, Great Britain controlled ninety percent of the world's diamond trade. Queen Victoria was the ruler of Great Britain during much of its imperialism. She ruled from 1837 to 1901.

The British controlled a lot of land and people in Africa. They also controlled India. India provided

The sepoys began to fight against the British in India in 1857.

Queen Victoria

Hawaii was an island colony of the United States.

raw materials to Great Britain. It was also a good place for British merchants to sell their goods. Great Britain made a lot of money by controlling India.

At first, India was controlled by a British trade company. The British used many Indians as servants. They made the Indians pay high taxes. They also had an army of Indian soldiers called **sepoys**. Then in 1857 the sepoys began to fight against the British trade company. The British won the war against the sepoys. At this time the British government took control of India. The British ruled India until 1947.

In some ways the British helped India. They built canals, railroads, bridges, and new buildings. But the Indians did not like being ruled by the British. They were forced to work hard at low-paying jobs. They were treated as a lower class of people in their own country. In many parts of India, there were signs that read "For Europeans only." The Indians were angry about this **discrimination**. Many Indians felt that they did not have any rights. Discrimination also happened in other European colonies.

The United States was also an imperialist nation. The United States ruled island colonies in the Pacific Ocean and in the Caribbean Sea. One island colony was Hawaii. The United States gained more colonies

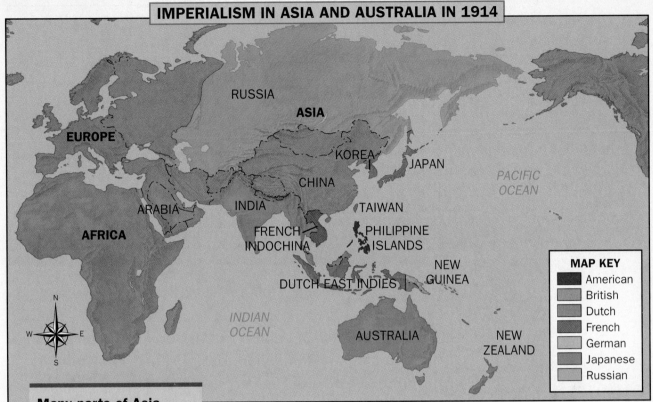

RUSSIA

ASIA

EUROPE

KOREA

JAPAN

CHINA

PACIFIC
OCEAN

ARABIA

INDIA

TAIWAN

AFRICA

FRENCH
INDOCHINA

PHILIPPINE
ISLANDS

NEW
GUINEA

DUTCH EAST INDIES

INDIAN
OCEAN

AUSTRALIA

NEW
ZEALAND

N
W E
S

MAP KEY
American
British
Dutch
French
German
Japanese
Russian

Many parts of Asia were controlled by imperialist nations. How many imperialist nations had colonies in Asia?

after winning the **Spanish-American War** in 1898. Puerto Rico and Guam were two of these colonies.

Many countries wanted to control the businesses and trade in Latin America. But the United States said that it would fight to prevent other nations from starting colonies in Latin America. In this way the United States protected its own interests in Latin American businesses.

Many nations wanted to control China, a large nation in Asia. China was able to make most of the goods it needed. So China did not want to trade with other countries. Europeans wanted to find something that the millions of Chinese people would want to buy. Finally, the British began to sell a drug called **opium** to the Chinese. Many Chinese wanted this dangerous drug. The Chinese government tried to stop the opium trade. This led to the **Opium War** between China and Great Britain in 1839. This war was fought mostly at sea. China lost the war because it could not defeat the powerful British navy.

The Opium War of 1839 was fought mostly at sea.

When four large United States ships came to Japan, the Japanese felt they had to agree to trade with the Americans.

Imperialist nations wanted to control China's trade.

Great Britain gained many trade rights in China. Soon other nations, including France, Germany, Japan, and Russia, controlled cities along China's coast. The United States wanted to trade in China. It encouraged open trade in China for all nations.

The Industrial Revolution did not reach Japan until the late 1800s. Japan did not want to trade with other countries. But in 1853, four large United States ships entered a Japanese harbor. Americans asked that Japan start to trade with the United States. The Japanese felt that they had to agree to trade with the Americans. But the Japanese did not want to be ruled by other nations. They decided to make Japan a modern industrial nation. Soon the Japanese built railroads, machines, and many factories. Japan also became an imperialist nation. The Japanese conquered parts of Asia in order to get raw materials for their factories.

Imperialism helped the imperialist nations gain raw materials and wealth. The people in the colonies were hurt by high taxes, low-paying jobs, and discrimination. Imperialism also caused wars. Nations fought one another to rule colonies. In 1914 a terrible war began in Europe. Why did this war begin? You will learn the answer in Chapter 6.

Using Vocabulary

Match Up   Finish the sentences in Group A with words from Group B. Write the letter of each correct answer on the blank line.

Group A

1. A nation that controls colonies or other nations is an _____ nation.

2. Indian soldiers that worked for a British trade company were called _____.

3. When a nation gains control over more land, it _____ its empire.

4. Laws that treat a group of people unfairly are examples of _____.

Group B

a. sepoys

b. expands

c. discrimination

d. imperialist

Read and Remember

Finish the Sentence   Draw a circle around the word or words that best complete each sentence.

1. Europeans used weapons and _____ to force Africans to work for them in mines and on plantations.

   canals   taxes   raw materials

2. The nation with the largest empire was _____.

   Great Britain   Japan   Portugal

3. By controlling _____, Great Britain controlled ninety percent of the world's diamond trade.

   India   Latin America   South Africa

4. The United States won the colonies of _____ during a war with Spain.

   Japan and China   Puerto Rico and Guam   India and South Africa

Write the Answer Write one or more sentences to answer each question.

1. What were four reasons that imperialism grew in the 1800s? _____

_____

_____

2. How did the United States protect its interests in Latin America?_____

_____

3. How did Japan change after 1853?_____

_____

Think and Apply

Fact or Opinion A **fact** is a true statement. An **opinion** is a statement that tells what a person thinks.

> **Fact** Wool is a raw material.
> **Opinion** Clothes that are made of wool are beautiful.

Write **F** next to each fact below. Write **O** next to each opinion. You should find two sentences that are opinions. The first one is done for you.

___F___ **1.** Nations such as France and Germany wanted to expand their empires during the late 1800s.

_____ **2.** Africa, Asia, Latin America, and the Middle East are rich in raw materials.

_____ **3.** It was not fair that the Indians were treated as a lower class of people in their own country.

_____ **4.** Queen Victoria was the greatest ruler in the world.

_____ **5.** The trade of a drug led to the Opium War of 1839 between Great Britain and China.

_____ **6.** The British built railroads and bridges in India.

Skill Builder

Using Map Keys   Sometimes a map uses different colors or symbols to show different things. A **map key** tells what those colors or symbols mean. Look at the map about imperialism in Asia and Australia on page 37. Study the map and the map key. Then write the answer to each question below.

1. What color shows the land controlled by Germans? _____

2. What are two nations on the map that were controlled by the British in 1914?

_____

3. Which nation controlled Korea? _____

4. Did France or Great Britain control more land in Asia? _____

5. Which land did the Dutch control? _____

Understanding a Political Cartoon   A **political cartoon** is a drawing that shows what an artist thinks about a certain person, event, or **issue**. An issue is an idea or a problem that people have different opinions about. Sometimes political cartoons seem funny, but they are usually about serious ideas. The political cartoon on page 38 is about imperialism. Study the political cartoon. Then circle or write the answer to each question below.

1. What nation does the pie represent?

   Russia   China   India

2. The people in the drawing are from different nations. What are they doing to the pie?

   dividing it   eating it   cooking it

3. The woman on the left is a woman you read about in this chapter. What is her name?

   Marie Curie   Empress Theodora   Queen Victoria

4. Do you think the artist was pleased about what the other nations were doing to China? Explain your answer on a separate piece of paper.

CHAPTER 6

World War I

THINK ABOUT AS YOU READ

1. **What were the causes of World War I?**
2. **Why did the United States enter the war?**
3. **What were some of the results of the war?**

NEW WORDS

- ◆ World War I
- ◆ military
- ◆ technology
- ◆ alliances
- ◆ tension
- ◆ neutral
- ◆ Central Powers
- ◆ submarines
- ◆ poison gas
- ◆ trenches
- ◆ surrendered
- ◆ Fourteen Points
- ◆ Treaty of Versailles
- ◆ League of Nations

PEOPLE & PLACES

- ◆ Archduke Francis Ferdinand
- ◆ Serbia
- ◆ Woodrow Wilson
- ◆ Edith Cavell
- ◆ Brussels

The late 1800s to the early 1900s was a time of great hope in Europe. Democracy was growing in some nations. The Industrial Revolution increased the food supply and helped people get jobs. Then in 1914 Austria-Hungary's Archduke Francis Ferdinand and his wife were shot by a person from Serbia. Suddenly many nations in Europe and other parts of the world were at war. This was the beginning of **World War I**. This war was also called the Great War.

The war was fought all over Europe. It was fought in Africa and in the Middle East. People from more than thirty nations fought in World War I. Millions of people were killed or wounded.

The deaths of the archduke and his wife were not the real causes of World War I. The four main causes began in the 1800s. Nationalism was one cause. People were united by pride for their nation. They wanted their nation to gain land, money, and power.

Airplanes were used for the first time in war during World War I.

The deaths of Austria-Hungary's archduke and his wife sparked World War I in 1914.

Kaiser Wilhelm II, the ruler of Germany during World War I

French soldiers during a battle in World War I

A second cause of World War I was an increase in **military** strength. Each nation wanted to be the strongest. The nations of Europe had built large armies. Germany had built the strongest army. Great Britain had built the strongest navy. But by 1898 Germany also had a strong navy. This made Germany a danger to Great Britain. By 1914 nations all over Europe had new military **technology**. New ships and weapons made the nations ready for war.

Imperialism was a third cause of World War I. The nations of Europe wanted more colonies. France was still angry that Germany had taken Alsace and Lorraine. France wanted these lands again. Serbia wanted land that was ruled by Austria-Hungary.

A fourth cause of World War I was that many nations had made **alliances**. This means that the nations had promised to fight for one another in a war. Austria-Hungary and Germany promised to fight for each other. Great Britain, France, and Russia also promised to help one another during a war.

These four causes created anger and **tension** between nations in Europe. So when Archduke Ferdinand was killed, Austria-Hungary went to war against Serbia. Then Germany promised to help

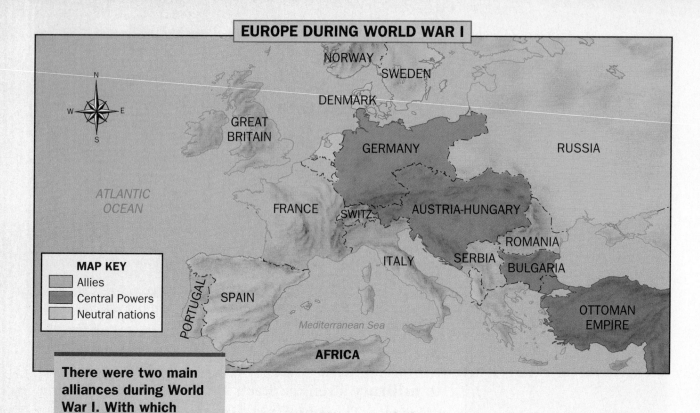

NORWAY
SWEDEN
DENMARK
GREAT BRITAIN
GERMANY
RUSSIA
ATLANTIC OCEAN
FRANCE
SWITZ.
AUSTRIA-HUNGARY
ROMANIA
ITALY
SERBIA
BULGARIA
PORTUGAL
SPAIN
Mediterranean Sea
OTTOMAN EMPIRE
AFRICA

MAP KEY
Allies
Central Powers
Neutral nations

There were two main alliances during World War I. With which alliance was Bulgaria?

ВСЕ ДЛЯ ВОЙНЫ!

ПОДПИСЬ

Women built weapons and machines during World War I.

Austria-Hungary fight. Russia said that it would help Serbia fight. So Germany declared war on Russia. Germany also declared war on its old enemy, France.

Then Germany invaded Belgium. Belgium was a **neutral** country. It did not want to fight in a war. Germany's attack on Belgium made Great Britain angry. Great Britain declared war on Germany. Soon there was fighting all over Europe. The fighting spread to Africa and the Middle East.

Germany and Austria-Hungary were the two main nations of an alliance called the **Central Powers**. Great Britain, Russia, France, Serbia, and many other nations were known as the Allies. There were also several neutral nations in Europe.

The Central Powers and the Allies both thought that they would win the war quickly. But the war did not end quickly. It lasted four years.

The German army fought in Russia and in France. In 1917 the Germans were winning in Russia. The Russians did not have enough guns. They did not have enough food. People in Russia had also begun a revolution. The Russians decided to stop fighting.

Soldiers from many nations fought in World War I. These Canadian soldiers are leaving a trench.

German submarine

Soldiers wore masks to avoid poison gas.

In 1917 the Russians signed a peace treaty with the Germans. Russia promised to stop helping the Allies.

New military technology was used during World War I. The Germans built new powerful ships called **submarines**. The German submarines could travel underwater to sneak up on and sink an enemy ship. The Germans also used **poison gas** to kill enemy soldiers. Airplanes, tanks, and new types of guns were also used for the first time in a war.

German soldiers fought the Allies in France for a long time. Soldiers fought one another from **trenches,** or long, deep ditches. Although millions of German soldiers and Allied soldiers were killed, neither side could defeat the other. The war also continued in other areas of Europe and Africa.

At first, Americans did not want to fight in World War I. Woodrow Wilson was the President of the United States during the war. He wanted the United States to be a neutral nation. But in 1915 Germany began to use its submarines to sink many ships that carried food and other goods to Great Britain. A submarine sank the *Lusitania*, a large British ship. More than a thousand people died, including 128 Americans. By 1917 the German navy had also sunk several American ships that were carrying goods to the Allies. Americans also found out that Germany

Many cities were completely destroyed during World War I.

Woodrow Wilson

A German submarine sank the *Lusitania* in 1915.

had tried to get Mexico to declare war on the United States. Wilson called for war against Germany. The United States entered World War I in April 1917.

American soldiers helped the Allies win World War I. The Allies and the Americans fought against the Germans in France. They also fought Austria-Hungary. At last in 1918, the Central Powers **surrendered** to the Allies. The war was over. The Allies had won.

Before the war was over, Wilson had begun to work for world peace. He had written a peace plan called the **Fourteen Points**. He wanted this plan to be used for the peace treaty after the war. These Fourteen Points told how German soldiers should leave Allied lands. The plan also included ways to prevent future wars. The Allies used some of the Fourteen Points when they wrote the **Treaty of Versailles** at the end of World War I.

The Treaty of Versailles punished Germany for its role in World War I. Germany had to pay billions of dollars to the Allies. Germany also lost some of its land and colonies. Another treaty punished Austria-Hungary. Austria-Hungary lost most of its land and became Austria. Austria and Germany were not allowed to have large armies and navies. The map on page 47 shows how Europe looked after World War I.

The Treaty of Versailles also started the **League of Nations**. President Wilson planned the League of

EUROPE AFTER WORLD WAR I

NORWAY
FINLAND
SWEDEN
DENMARK
GREAT BRITAIN
ATLANTIC OCEAN
GERMANY
POLAND
SOVIET UNION (U.S.S.R.)
LORRAINE
ALSACE
CZECHOSLOVAKIA
SWITZ.
AUSTRIA
HUNGARY
FRANCE
ROMANIA
YUGOSLAVIA
BULGARIA
ITALY
PORTUGAL
SPAIN
Mediterranean Sea
TURKEY
AFRICA

The size and names of many nations changed at the end of the war. Compare this map to the map on page 44. What happened to the nation of Austria-Hungary?

Leaders at the signing of the Treaty of Versailles

Nations when he wrote the Fourteen Points. The League was a group of nations that worked for world peace. It began in 1920 with 42 nations. The United States did not join the League. Many Americans believed that by joining the League they might have to fight in another war.

After World War I, the countries of the world faced new problems. Millions of people had been killed or wounded during the war. Some cities and towns had been completely destroyed. Many people in Europe were left without jobs, homes, or money. European countries needed money for new buildings and roads. But many nations had spent most of their money on the war. Many countries had borrowed money to pay for their weapons and armies. After the war, these nations could not pay back the money they had borrowed.

The Treaty of Versailles made many people angry. The treaty made the Germans hate the Allies. The Germans wanted their nation to be strong again. Would the Germans live in peace with the Allies? You will find the answer in Chapters 8 and 9.

Edith Cavell (1865–1915)

Women were not soldiers in World War I, but they played a very important part in the war. Many worked in factories to build weapons. Others became nurses to help care for wounded soldiers. One of the greatest World War I nurses was Edith Cavell.

Edith Cavell was born in England in 1865. For her first job, she moved to Belgium where she cared for a family's children. While she was in Belgium, her father became ill. Cavell returned to England to help nurse her father back to health. Cavell realized that she enjoyed nursing.

Edith Cavell

In 1895 Cavell was accepted by the London Hospital in England to be trained as a nurse. After that she worked as a nurse in England for several years. In 1907 Cavell became the head nurse in a teaching hospital in Brussels, Belgium. She started the nursing system in Belgium.

Soon after World War I began, German soldiers took control of the city of Brussels. Edith Cavell began working to help Allied soldiers escape from Belgium to Holland, a neutral nation. Cavell nursed injured soldiers and let them hide in the hospital until they were well enough to leave. Then the soldiers were given money and a guide to show them their escape route.

Cavell with nurses during World War I

Within a few months, Cavell had helped several hundred soldiers escape. However, Cavell was caught by the Germans. On October 12, 1915, the Germans executed her for helping the Allied soldiers.

After the war, Cavell's body was brought back to England and buried there. A statue was built in London to honor Cavell. Many books have been written about Edith Cavell. People still admire this fine nurse for her courage during World War I.

Using Vocabulary

Find the Meaning   Write on the blank the word or words that best complete each sentence.

1. The **Central Powers** was an alliance that included Austria-Hungary and

_____.

Great Britain   Serbia   Germany

2. A **neutral** nation is a nation that does not want to _____.

fight in a war   lose   win

3. Soldiers in World War I fought in **trenches,** or long _____.

submarines   tanks   ditches

4. To **surrender** means to _____.

fight   give up   win

5. The **League of Nations** was a group that worked for _____.

world peace   military technology   wars

Read and Remember

Find the Answer   Put a check (✔) next to each sentence that gives one of the causes of World War I. You should check four sentences.

_____ **1.** Nationalism was strong in many nations.

_____ **2.** Many nations in Europe wanted to expand their empires.

_____ **3.** The League of Nations was part of Woodrow Wilson's Fourteen Points.

_____ **4.** Many nations had made alliances with one another.

_____ **5.** The Industrial Revolution increased the supply of food and jobs.

_____ **6.** German submarines sank the *Lusitania*.

_____ **7.** Many nations were increasing their military strength with new technology.

Finish the Paragraphs   Use the words in dark print to finish the paragraphs below. Write on the correct blank lines the words you choose.

> **Versailles**   **neutral**   **Ferdinand**   **technology**
> **tension**   **Allies**   **Serbia**   **Germany**

There was much _____ between nations in 1914. That is why the deaths of Archduke _____ and his wife sparked World War I. When Austria-Hungary declared war on _____, the allies of the two nations also began to fight. The two alliances in World War I were the Central Powers and the _____. New war _____ included submarines, tanks, airplanes, and poison gas.

At first, Americans wanted the United States to be _____. Then in 1917 the United States declared war on _____. The Americans helped the Allies win the war in 1918. The leaders of the Allies wrote the Treaty of _____, which punished Germany.

Skill Builder

Reading a Historical Map   A **historical map** shows information about events and places during a certain time period. The historical map on page 44 shows the Central Powers, the Allies, and the neutral countries in Europe during World War I. Study the map and the map key. Then write the answer to each question.

1. What color is used to show the Allies? _____

2. What were two nations that were part of the Central Powers? _____

_____

3. What were two nations that were part of the Allies? _____

_____

4. Was Romania a neutral country? _____

5. Was Switzerland allied with France? _____

Journal Writing

 Write a paragraph that explains why people honor Edith Cavell for her courage.

Think and Apply

Cause and Effect   A **cause** is something that makes something else happen. What happens is called the **effect**.

> **Cause**   Japan did not want to be ruled by other nations.
> **Effect**   Japan decided to become a modern industrial nation.

Match each cause on the left with an effect on the right. Write the letter of the effect on the correct blank. The first one is done for you.

Cause

1. Each nation in Europe wanted to be the strongest, so ___b___

2. Russia did not have enough food and weapons, so _____

3. German submarines kept sinking American ships, so _____

4. Germany knew it could not win World War I, so _____

5. Many cities were completely destroyed during World War I, so _____

6. Nations had spent most of their money during the war, so _____

Effect

a. many people in Europe did not have homes after the war.

b. the nations built strong armies and navies.

c. in 1918 it surrendered to the Allies.

d. the United States went to war against Germany.

e. after the war they could not pay back the money they had borrowed.

f. it signed a peace treaty with Germany in 1917.

CHAPTER 7

Revolutions in Russia

Russia is the world's largest country in size. It covers parts of Europe and Asia. The Industrial Revolution that changed Western Europe did not come to Russia until the 1860s. Most Russians remained poor farmers. They had to obey absolute rulers. These rulers were called **czars**. In 1917 Russia had two major revolutions. After the revolutions, Russia was no longer ruled by a czar. Why did these revolutions happen?

In the years before 1917, many Russians were unhappy. They had little freedom. Most people were peasants called **serfs**. The serfs worked on land that belonged to nobles. The serfs were not free. They were often treated very cruelly. They did not have enough food. They could not go to school to learn to read and write. Some peasants became factory

Vladimir Lenin and the Bolsheviks led the Russian Revolution of 1917.

Russian peasants were forced to work as slaves. These serfs are using hammers to crush rocks between their feet.

workers. They were paid very low wages. Most of the peasants were very hungry.

The czars made all the laws. Many czars were very cruel. They were often hated by their people. There was no freedom of speech. Some czars made a few changes to improve life for the peasants. One czar freed the serfs. But the serfs were not given any land. The czars also involved Russia in several wars. Many Russians were killed during the wars.

Some people tried to start revolutions in order to change Russia. The revolutions that took place before 1917 failed to bring changes to Russia.

A group of Russians called the Bolsheviks wanted Russia to become a **Communist** nation. They used many ideas from a German named Karl Marx. In 1848 Karl Marx wrote a book about **communism**. He said that workers should start a revolution against business owners. Marx said that workers would be the rulers in a Communist government. Marx's ideas brought new hope to Russia's poor, hungry peasants. The peasants believed that a Communist government would improve life for them.

In 1894 Nicholas II became Russia's czar. During his rule, people continued to be poor and unhappy. Many peasants starved because of bad crops. Factory workers wanted better wages and better working conditions. In 1905 thousands of workers went to

Czar Nicholas II with his son Alexis

the czar's palace to ask for changes. Government soldiers shot hundreds of these workers. People were very angry. Soon revolutions began all over Russia. But Nicholas II continued to rule Russia. He refused to make changes to help the poor.

Then World War I began. The Russians fought against the Central Powers. Almost two million Russian soldiers died during the war. Railroads carried military supplies and food to the Russian soldiers. But at home the Russian people were starving. The Russian people wanted peace. But the czar would not let Russia leave the war. Russian soldiers continued to fight and die.

In March 1917 an important revolution began in Russia. Angry Russians began to march and riot in the streets of Petrograd, Russia's capital city. Other Russians began to strike. People demanded bread. They wanted coal to heat their homes. They wanted Russia to stop fighting in World War I. Nicholas II lost his control of Russia. He was forced to leave his position as czar. He and his family were then put in prison. Later, they were executed by the Bolsheviks. Nicholas II was the last czar of Russia.

A new government controlled Russia after the March revolution. A parliament was started. The new government was weak. People were still poor and hungry. Russian soldiers continued to die in World War I. People became unhappy with the new government. Another revolution began in November. This was the **Russian Revolution** of 1917. It was started by the Bolsheviks.

A man named Vladimir Lenin led the Bolsheviks during the Russian Revolution. Lenin promised to give the Russians peace, land, and bread. These were the three things the Russians wanted. The Bolsheviks captured the capital city of Petrograd. They soon controlled the Russian government. Lenin was the leader of the government. In 1918 the city of Moscow became the capital of Russia.

Vladimir Lenin

The Soviet Union was formed in 1922. What were two cities in the Soviet Union?

SOVIET UNION (U.S.S.R.)

Leningrad

Moscow

URAL MOUNTAINS

Volga River

Ob River

EUROPE

ASIA

AFRICA

PACIFIC OCEAN

INDIAN OCEAN

N W E S

A poster asking people to join the Bolsheviks

As soon as Lenin became ruler, he took Russia out of World War I. Lenin ruled as a dictator. He had full power to make laws. Lenin's government took control of most farms and factories. The government also took away the power of Russia's church.

Many Russians did not want the new government. Some of them wanted Russia to be ruled by a czar again. These people were called White Russians. The White Russians began to fight against the Bolsheviks. A **civil war** began. During a civil war, people of the same nation fight against one another. The civil war lasted three years. In 1920 the Bolsheviks won.

In 1922 the Bolsheviks created a new Communist nation. They called the new nation the Union of Soviet Socialist Republics, or U.S.S.R. It was also called the Soviet Union. The Soviet Union was the union of Russia and many small republics. The Bolsheviks called themselves the Communist party.

Lenin ruled the Soviet Union until he died in 1924. By that time the government owned most farms and industries. Lenin had promised to give land to the peasants. But the peasants never got their land. The government owned the land. Lenin had promised more food. But for many years there was not enough food in the Soviet Union.

Joseph Stalin was the dictator of the Soviet Union for 25 years.

People on a collective farm in the Soviet Union

Flag of the Soviet Union

Joseph Stalin became the next dictator of the Soviet Union. He made the Soviet Union a major world power. Stalin built a powerful army. Many factories were also built. During Stalin's rule, most people worked together on large **collective farms** that were owned by the government. But there was still not enough food.

Joseph Stalin ruled for 25 years. His government had total control of life in the Soviet Union. People were told not to believe in any religion. Many people were afraid of Stalin. His secret police **arrested** many people who spoke out against his government. Millions of people in the Soviet Union were killed or sent to prison by Stalin.

Many people fight revolutions to get freedom. The American and French revolutions in the 1700s were fought for freedom. But the Russian Revolution of 1917 did not bring freedom to the people of Russia. The revolution only changed the absolute rulers of Russia from czars to dictators. Communists ruled the Soviet Union for almost seventy years. But many people in the Soviet Union did not like communism. In Chapter 19 you will learn how communism ended in the Soviet Union.

Karl Marx (1818–1883)

Karl Marx was a German who had many ideas about government and workers. His ideas were used to bring Communist governments to many nations.

Marx was born in 1818 in what was then Prussia. At college he studied history, government, and law. He also studied different ways of thinking. He shared many ideas with teachers and students who did not like the government of Prussia.

Karl Marx became a writer. He wrote about governments and businesses. He also wrote about bad working conditions in factories. Marx believed that business owners unfairly used working-class people to gain wealth. He said that in this way rich people became richer and poor people became poorer. Marx believed that the differences between the rich and the poor led to problems. He thought that problems would end if people were no longer divided into classes.

Karl Marx

Marx and a close friend wrote about these ideas in a short book called *The Communist Manifesto*. In this book the two men told the working class to start a revolution against the ruling class. They wrote that businesses should be owned by all workers. All people should share wealth. Then there would be very few rich people or poor people. Many people, including the Bolsheviks in Russia, used Marx's ideas to start revolutions in their nations.

Marx's ideas were used to develop communism. Communism is a system that allows the government to own all farms and industries. Many nations used Marx's ideas to form Communist governments. In this way Karl Marx affected governments, businesses, and people in countries all over the world.

Using Vocabulary

Finish Up   Choose the word or words in dark print to best complete each sentence. Write the word or words on the correct blank line.

communism   Russian Revolution   collective   czars

1. After the year 1500, the rulers of Russia were called _____.

2. Under the system of _____, the government owns all farms and industries.

3. During Stalin's rule, most people worked together on large farms called

_____ farms.

4. The _____ was fought in 1917 because people in Russia were unhappy with the new government.

Read and Remember

Choose the Answer   Draw a circle around the correct answer.

1. Who was Russia's last czar?

Nicholas II   Vladimir Lenin   Joseph Stalin

2. Who did Karl Marx say would be the rulers in a Communist government?

czars   presidents   workers

3. Which group wanted Russia to become a Communist nation?

Bolsheviks   White Russians   Germans

4. Which leader took Russia out of World War I?

Nicholas II   Vladimir Lenin   Joseph Stalin

Journal Writing

Pretend you are Karl Marx. Write a short letter to a friend. Tell your friend how you feel about businesses and workers.

Think and Apply

Drawing Conclusions   Read each pair of sentences. Then look in the box for the conclusion you might make. Write the letter of the conclusion on the blank line.

1. Russian peasants often did not have enough food.
Russian factory workers were paid very low wages.

Conclusion _____

2. The Russian people hated the czar.
The Russian people wanted changes.

Conclusion _____

3. Almost two million Russian soldiers were killed in World War I.
People in Russia were starving during the war because the food supplies
   were being sent to soldiers.

Conclusion _____

4. After the Russian Revolution, the Bolsheviks ruled Russia.
The White Russians wanted a czar to rule Russia.

Conclusion _____

5. Millions of people in the Soviet Union were killed or were sent to prison
   by Stalin.
People were arrested if they spoke out against Stalin.

Conclusion _____

> **a.** People in the Soviet Union were afraid of Stalin.
> **b.** Life was hard for peasants and factory workers in Russia.
> **c.** They began to fight in a civil war.
> **d.** People wanted Russia to stop fighting in the war.
> **e.** The Russian people began a revolution.

Crossword Puzzle

Each sentence below has a word missing. Choose the missing word for each sentence from the words in dark print. Then write the words in the correct places on the puzzle.

─────────────────── **ACROSS** ───────────────────

government   Lenin   Stalin   bread

1. The Russian people wanted peace, land, and _____ .

2. The Soviet _____ owned most farms and factories.

3. As dictator, Joseph _____ helped the Soviet Union build a powerful army.

4. _____ was the leader of the Bolsheviks.

─────────────────── **DOWN** ───────────────────

workers   czar   police   civil

5. Stalin's secret _____ arrested many people who spoke out against the dictator.

6. Before 1917 the _____ made all the laws in Russia.

7. Karl Marx said that businesses should be owned by all _____ .

8. During a _____ war, people of the same nation fight one another.

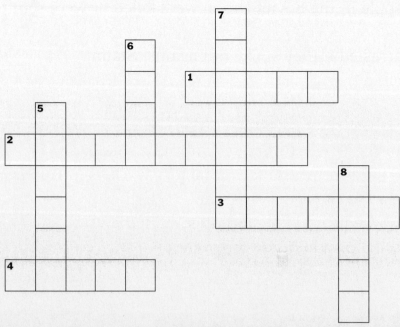

The Rise of Dictators

Europe had many problems after World War I. The war had cost nations millions of dollars. Millions of people did not have jobs, homes, or enough food. Italy, Germany, and other nations were angry about the Treaty of Versailles. People began to want strong leaders. In some nations, people believed that dictators could solve their problems.

You have read about Lenin and Stalin in the Soviet Union. Lenin gained strong control of the nation during his rule. Stalin was also a strong dictator. He increased the industries and the military strength of the Soviet Union. By the 1930s the Soviet Union was a major world power.

THINK ABOUT AS YOU READ

1. How did dictators gain power after World War I?
2. How did the Great Depression affect nations in Europe and Asia?
3. Why did Italy, Germany, and Japan build large armies?

NEW WORDS

♦ Great Depression
♦ concentration camps
♦ Axis Powers

PEOPLE & PLACES

♦ Benito Mussolini
♦ Ethiopia
♦ Adolf Hitler
♦ Nazis
♦ General Hideki Tojo
♦ Czechoslovakia

The 1930s brought new dictators to power. Mussolini and Hitler wanted their nations to be great empires.

Benito Mussolini

Germans selling tin cans during the 1929 depression

Adolf Hitler

During World War I, Italy had fought with the Allies against Germany. Like many European countries, Italy had money problems after the war. The people of Italy were also angry that their country did not gain much land from the Treaty of Versailles. They turned to a man named Benito Mussolini to solve their problems. Mussolini helped the growth of nationalism in Italy. He promised to help Italy become a great empire. People in Italy believed that Mussolini would help them.

In 1922 Benito Mussolini became Italy's dictator. Mussolini made all the laws. Soon the people of Italy had no freedom. Workers were not allowed to strike. Newspapers were censored. Mussolini's secret police arrested people who spoke out against the dictator. Some people were killed.

Mussolini wanted to conquer new land for Italy. He built a large army and prepared his nation for war. In 1935 Mussolini conquered Ethiopia, a country in Africa. The Allies and the League of Nations were angry with Mussolini for attacking Ethiopia. But they did nothing to stop Mussolini. They did not want another world war to begin.

In 1929 the **Great Depression** began in the United States. A depression is a time when business becomes very slow. A depression can last many years. During the Great Depression, many banks, factories, and other businesses closed. Millions of people lost their jobs and all of their money. This terrible depression soon spread to many parts of the world.

The Great Depression brought very hard times to Germany. The nation already had many money problems because of the Treaty of Versailles. The treaty said that Germany must pay a very large amount of money to the Allies. But Germany did not have enough money to do this. People in Germany were poor. Many people were starving. By 1933 the depression was very bad in Germany. Factories and banks closed. Almost half of the working people did

Hitler often spoke to thousands of his soldiers to encourage them to fight for Germany.

Nazi soldiers

Secret police arrested many Jews in Germany.

not have jobs. People did not have money to buy food. The Germans blamed the Allies and the Treaty of Versailles for their many problems. They wanted Germany to be strong again.

Adolf Hitler knew that the German people were very unhappy. Hitler was the leader of a group of Germans called the Nazis. The Nazis had their own army. Hitler told the German people that he would make new jobs. He said that he would help Germany conquer and rule the world. Many Germans liked Hitler's ideas. He made people feel very proud to be Germans. Nationalism grew stronger in Germany. Many German people wanted Hitler and the Nazis to rule Germany.

In 1933 Adolf Hitler became Germany's dictator. He had complete power. The Nazis worked to keep Hitler as their nation's dictator. Soon there was no freedom at all in Hitler's Germany. The Nazis controlled all activities in Germany. They controlled newspapers, radios, literature, music, and art. There was no freedom of speech. Secret police arrested people who spoke out or wrote against the ideas of Hitler. Many people were sent to prisons called **concentration camps**.

Hitler believed that Germans were better than all other people in the world. He also strongly hated

Jews. In 1935 he said that Jews were no longer German citizens. Jews were no longer allowed to work in hospitals, banks, or many other places. Nazis beat many Jews and burned Jewish homes and temples. Many Jews were arrested and sent to concentration camps.

Hitler knew that most Germans were angry about the Treaty of Versailles. The Germans wanted to have a large, powerful army again. They wanted to rule all the land that had been part of the German Empire. The treaty would not let Germany do these things. Hitler said that he would not obey the treaty. He planned ways to make Germany strong again.

Japanese soldiers

Hitler secretly built a strong German army. He had German factories make many weapons. The factories made guns, tanks, and airplanes. Soon Germany was ready for war.

While Italy and Germany prepared for war, Japan also prepared for war. Japan was a strong nation after World War I. There had not been any fighting on Japanese land during the war. Japan's trade and industries had grown. Japan was the most powerful country in Asia. Nationalism in Japan grew. Military leaders took control of Japan's government.

The depression that had begun in 1929 hurt the Japanese. People in other countries did not have money to buy Japan's goods. Many factories and other businesses in Japan closed. Many people lost their jobs. Farmers could not sell their crops.

Hideki Tojo

Japanese military leaders decided that Japan should conquer other nations in Asia. These nations would give Japan many raw materials and new places to sell goods. Japan's General Hideki Tojo strongly encouraged war. He and the other military leaders told the Japanese people that war would be good for Japan. Many Japanese trained to become soldiers. In 1931 the Japanese army attacked and conquered part of China. The League of Nations did little to stop Japan.

The Japanese invaded China in 1937.

MAP KEY
Axis nations
Axis-controlled lands

GREAT BRITAIN
GERMANY POLAND
CZECHOSLOVAKIA
FRANCE
AUSTRIA
ITALY
SPAIN
ALBANIA
Mediterranean Sea

The Axis Powers in Europe in 1938

Nazi soldiers entering Prague, Czechoslovakia

Italy, Germany, and Japan built strong armies. They all hoped to expand their empires. In 1936 they formed an alliance. Germany, Italy, and Japan were called the **Axis Powers**. They agreed to help one another conquer other lands.

The Axis Powers tested their strength by fighting in a civil war in Spain in 1937. The same year Japan began a major attack on China. In 1938 Hitler was ready for Germany to conquer Europe. That year German soldiers went to Austria. The Austrians did not fight. They allowed Austria to be ruled by Hitler.

Then Hitler's soldiers took control of part of Czechoslovakia. Great Britain and France were angry. Hitler promised these two nations that he would not try to take over the rest of Czechoslovakia. Then later Hitler went against this agreement. He took control of all of Czechoslovakia. This might have started a major war. But Great Britain and France did not want another world war. To keep peace, they decided to allow Hitler to conquer Czechoslovakia. They hoped that this would keep Hitler from wanting to conquer other nations.

The Axis Powers continued to gain strength. They began to look at other lands to conquer. Soon Great Britain and France realized that Hitler and his allies would not keep peace. They began to prepare for war.

Using Vocabulary

Match Up   Finish the sentences in Group A with words from Group B. Write the letter of each correct answer on the blank line.

Group A

1. The _____ was the period after 1929 when many businesses and people lost all of their money.

2. In 1936 Germany, Italy, and Japan formed an alliance called the _____.

3. The Nazis forced many people to go to prisons called _____.

Group B

a. Axis Powers

b. concentration camps

c. Great Depression

Journal Writing

Hitler and Mussolini were very powerful dictators in Europe. Write a paragraph that tells at least three ways these dictators were alike.

Read and Remember

Finish Up   Choose the word in dark print that best completes each sentence. Write the word on the correct blank line.

Ethiopia   citizens   money   Asia   Versailles

1. After World War I, many nations needed _____.

2. Mussolini's soldiers conquered _____ for Italy in 1935.

3. Hitler knew that the people of Germany were angry about the Treaty of

_____.

4. Hitler said that Jews were no longer German _____.

5. Japan decided that it could solve its problems by conquering land in

_____.

Who Am I?   Read each sentence. Then look at the words in dark print for the name of the person who might have said it. Write on the blank after each sentence the name of the person you choose.

Joseph Stalin   Adolf Hitler   Benito Mussolini
Vladimir Lenin   Hideki Tojo

1. "I was the first dictator in Russia after the revolution of 1917."

   _____

2. "As dictator of Italy, I prepared the nation for war." _____

3. "I was one of the Japanese military leaders who led Japan to attack China in

   the 1930s." _____

4. "After Lenin died, I helped the Soviet Union increase its industries and

   become a world power." _____

5. "I was the German dictator who led the Nazis to conquer Austria and

   Czechoslovakia." _____

Think and Apply

Categories   Read the words in each group. Decide how they are alike. Find the best title for each group from the words in dark print. Write the title on the line above each group.

Japan   Great Depression   Dictators   Nazis

1. _____
   Hitler
   Mussolini
   Stalin

2. _____
   hurt nations all over the world
   millions of people lost money
   factories and banks closed

3. _____
   kept Hitler in power
   arrested Jews
   controlled newspapers

4. _____
   Asian nation
   military leaders
   attacked China

Unit 3 World War II and Its Effects

People in many parts of the world wanted peace after World War I. The League of Nations was started to keep peace between nations. But the League of Nations could not stop nations from building strong armies. The League could not stop Italy, Germany, and Japan from starting the next world war.

World War II was the most terrible war the world had ever seen. More nations fought in this war than in any other war. More people died in this war than in any other war. The most powerful weapon ever invented was used during World War II. Nations learned that they would have to find new ways to keep peace.

The years after 1945 brought important changes to the world. A new, stronger peace-keeping organization was started after World War II. The United States and the Soviet Union became very powerful nations. Soon after the war, Communist leaders took control of many governments. The United States and other democracies tried to stop countries from becoming Communist nations. Sometimes wars were fought. But the nations were careful not to have another world war.

PACIFIC OCEAN

ATLANTIC OCEAN

PACIFIC OCEAN

INDIAN OCEAN

How did the Allies win World War II? What was the Cold War? How are nations working for peace? As you read Unit 3, think about how differences in governments can lead to wars. Think about how World War II, the Cold War, and the Vietnam War affected the world.

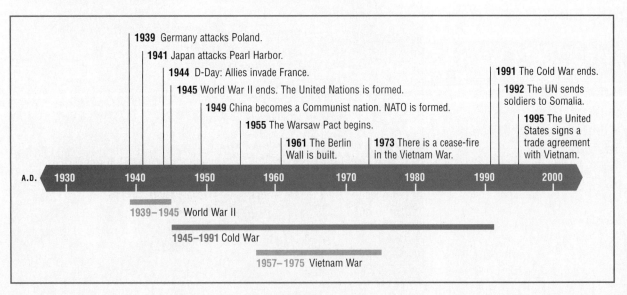

1939 Germany attacks Poland.

1941 Japan attacks Pearl Harbor.

1944 D-Day: Allies invade France.

1945 World War II ends. The United Nations is formed.

1949 China becomes a Communist nation. NATO is formed.

1955 The Warsaw Pact begins.

1961 The Berlin Wall is built.

1973 There is a cease-fire in the Vietnam War.

1991 The Cold War ends.

1992 The UN sends soldiers to Somalia.

1995 The United States signs a trade agreement with Vietnam.

A.D. | 1930 | 1940 | 1950 | 1960 | 1970 | 1980 | 1990 | 2000

1939–1945 World War II

1945–1991 Cold War

1957–1975 Vietnam War

The Beginning of World War II

Great Britain and France wanted peace after World War I. But Adolf Hitler wanted war. He wanted Germany to rule the world. The other Axis Powers wanted to rule the world with Germany. Italy wanted to rule land in Europe and Africa. Japan wanted to rule Asia. Later, other countries would join the Axis Powers.

Great Britain and France were called the Allies. The Allies did not want to fight in another war. This is why the two nations allowed Hitler to conquer Austria and Czechoslovakia. Hitler promised that he would not conquer any more nations. He broke that promise. In 1939 Germany invaded Poland. This time the Allies said that they would fight for Poland. Great Britain and France declared war against Germany. **World War II** had begun.

THINK ABOUT AS YOU READ

1. **Why did Germany, Italy, and Japan want another war?**
2. **Why did Germany lose the Battle of Britain?**
3. **What caused the United States to fight in World War II?**

NEW WORDS

- **World War II**
- **Battle of Britain**
- **bombs**
- **bombed**
- **Battle of Stalingrad**
- **naval base**

PEOPLE & PLACES

- **Poland**
- **Dunkirk**
- **Winston Churchill**
- **Soviets**
- **Franklin D. Roosevelt**
- **Pearl Harbor**

Hitler salutes his soldiers as they march into Poland in 1939.

Allied soldiers wading out to boats at Dunkirk, France

Winston Churchill

The city of London during the Battle of Britain

The German army was strong. They conquered Poland in a few weeks. Then the German soldiers conquered northern Europe. In 1940 they attacked France. British soldiers and French soldiers fought the Germans in France.

Soon the Allies realized that France would be conquered. The British soldiers and French soldiers who were fighting there did not want to be captured. Great Britain sent hundreds of ships and small boats to Dunkirk, France, to help the soldiers escape. Thousands of soldiers went to Great Britain in the boats. These Allied soldiers would continue to fight against Hitler.

Germany conquered France. By 1940 the Axis Powers had conquered most of Europe. Then Adolf Hitler decided to conquer Great Britain. The prime minister of Great Britain was Winston Churchill. Winston Churchill said that Great Britain would never surrender to Hitler. Churchill was a strong leader. He gave the people of Great Britain hope that they could defeat the Germans.

The German fight against Great Britain was called the **Battle of Britain**. German airplanes dropped **bombs** on British cities. Germany **bombed** Great Britain for many months. Many people were killed. Many buildings were destroyed. But the British were brave. They did not surrender to the Germans. Great Britain's Royal Air Force shot down more than 2,000 German planes. Finally in 1941, the Germans stopped attacking Great Britain from the air. The battle was over. But World War II continued.

Other nations became involved in World War II. Six of these nations joined the Axis Powers. By the end of the war, almost 50 nations had joined the Allies. But the Axis Powers were very strong. They conquered most of Europe and parts of Asia and Africa. The Axis nations were winning World War II.

Then Hitler decided that the Soviet Union was an enemy. Hitler also wanted oil and wheat from the

EUROPE DURING WORLD WAR II

MAP KEY

- Axis nation
- Area under Axis control
- Neutral nation
- Allied nation
- ✳ Battle
- ● City

NORWAY, SWEDEN, FINLAND, GREAT BRITAIN, DENMARK, ● Moscow, SOVIET UNION (U.S.S.R.), Berlin, ATLANTIC OCEAN, London ●, GERMANY, POLAND, Dunkirk, ● Paris, CZECHOSLOVAKIA, ✳ Stalingrad, FRANCE, SWITZ., AUSTRIA, HUNGARY, ROMANIA, YUGOSLAVIA, BULGARIA, ITALY, ALBANIA, SPAIN, GREECE, TURKEY, Mediterranean Sea, ALGERIA, LIBYA, EGYPT ✳

The Axis Powers conquered most of Europe during World War II. Was Yugoslavia an area under Axis control?

Italian airplanes and British airplanes in battle above Egypt

Soviet Union. In 1941 Germany attacked the Soviet Union. This attack forced the Soviets to fight against the Germans. So the Soviet Union joined the Allies.

At first, the Germans won many battles in the Soviet Union. But the Soviets fought back. They remembered how they had fought Napoleon in 1812. They had burned their own farms and houses to defeat Napoleon. The Soviets did almost the same thing during World War II. They decided to burn everything the Germans might use. The Soviets burned houses, factories, and food. Then winter came. The weather was very cold. Snow covered the land. The Germans did not have enough food or warm clothing. Many Germans died. Then at the **Battle of Stalingrad** in 1943, the last Germans in the Soviet Union surrendered.

There was also fighting in the Atlantic Ocean. German submarines sank many ships that carried food, weapons, and other supplies to the British. But World War II brought new technology. Some of this new technology helped the Allies locate many of the German submarines that were underwater. When

On December 7, 1941, the Japanese dropped bombs on Pearl Harbor. The event brought the United States into World War II.

Franklin D. Roosevelt

Pearl Harbor, Hawaii

the submarines came up to the top of the water, the Allies dropped bombs on them from airplanes.

Across the Atlantic Ocean, the United States was a neutral nation. It did not want to fight in World War II. But Americans helped the Allies in other ways. Franklin D. Roosevelt was the President of the United States. He had American factories make weapons, tanks, and planes. American farmers grew extra food. The United States sent the food and weapons to Great Britain, the Soviet Union, and other Allies.

Americans hoped that they would not have to fight in World War II. But in 1941 General Hideki Tojo became the main military leader of Japan. On December 7, 1941, Tojo ordered Japanese soldiers to attack Pearl Harbor in the Pacific Ocean. Pearl Harbor was a large American **naval base** in Hawaii. The Japanese destroyed American ships and planes. They killed more than 2,000 Americans.

The people in the United States were very angry. They knew it was time for war. The next day, the United States declared war against Japan. Three days later, Germany and Italy declared war against the United States. Americans would help the Allies fight against the Axis Powers in Asia and in Europe.

Nations all over the world were now fighting in World War II. The war would continue for four more years. Who would win World War II? How would the war end? Read the next chapter to find out.

Using Vocabulary

Analogies An **analogy** compares two pairs of words. The words in the first pair are alike in the same way as the words in the second pair. For example, **Great Britain** is to **Allies** as **Germany** is to **Axis Powers**. Use the words in dark print to best complete the sentences. The first one is done for you.

bomb   **naval base**   **Battle of Britain**   **World War II**

1. Central Powers is to World War I as Axis Powers is to ___World War II___.

2. Airport is to airplane as _____ is to navy ships.

3. Japan is to the attack on Pearl Harbor as Germany is to the

_____.

4. Submarine is to ship underwater as _____ is to exploding weapon.

Read and Remember

Write the Answer Write one or more sentences to answer each question.

1. What did Hitler do that caused World War II to begin? _____

_____

2. What happened at Dunkirk, France? _____

_____

_____

3. How did the British win the Battle of Britain? _____

_____

4. How did the Soviets stop the German soldiers from conquering the Soviet

Union? _____

_____

5. How did the United States help the Allies while it was a neutral nation?

_____

_____

6. Why did the United States enter World War II? _____

_____

Skill Builder

Reading a Bar Graph   A **bar graph** shows facts using bars of different lengths. The bar graph below shows how many soldiers different countries sent to fight in World War II. The bar graph also uses colors to show whether the nations were part of the Allies or part of the Axis Powers. Study the bar graph. Then write the answer to each question.

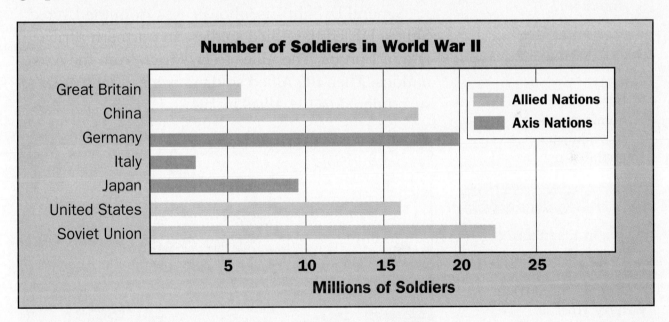

1. What color are the bars that show Allied nations?_____

2. Which country sent the fewest soldiers to the war? _____

3. Which country sent the most soldiers?_____

4. About how many soldiers did Great Britain send to the war?_____

5. About how many total soldiers did the three Axis Powers send? _____

CHAPTER 10

The End of World War II

THINK ABOUT AS YOU READ

1. How did the Allies free France?
2. Why did Germany finally surrender?
3. How did the United States force Japan to surrender?

NEW WORDS

- D-Day
- Holocaust
- atomic bomb
- isolationism
- rebuild

PEOPLE & PLACES

- Dwight Eisenhower
- Normandy
- Philippines
- Douglas MacArthur
- Harry Truman
- Hiroshima
- Nagasaki
- Anne Frank
- Jewish Germans

The Axis Powers had been winning World War II when the United States entered the war. The Battle of Stalingrad in 1943 marked an important change in the war. After this battle, the Allies began to win World War II.

Great Britain, the United States, and the Soviet Union worked hard to create a plan to defeat the Axis Powers in Europe. First, they planned to push the Germans and the Italians from northern Africa. From Africa, the Allies would conquer Italy. Then they would invade France. Their plan worked.

General Dwight Eisenhower was from the United States. He led the Allied soldiers in northern Africa and in Europe. The Allies freed Africa from the Axis nations. Then the Allied soldiers went to Italy. Italy surrendered to the Allies in 1943.

Allied soldiers were welcomed by the French people after the soldiers defeated the Germans at Normandy.

MAP KEY
- Area under Axis control
- Allied area
- Neutral nation
- ← Allied attack
- ✶ Battle
- • City

The Allies worked hard to plan a way to defeat the Axis Powers. To which nation did most of their routes of attack finally lead?

Dwight Eisenhower

The Allies planned to free France from Germany. General Eisenhower led the Allied soldiers in these attacks. On June 6, 1944, the Allies invaded France. This important date is known as **D-Day**. On D-Day, thousands of Allied soldiers sailed from Great Britain across the English Channel. They landed on the beaches of Normandy, an area of northern France.

The Allies surprised the Germans in France on D-Day. But the Germans fought hard against the Allies. Thousands of soldiers died. The Allies fought their way through France. In August the Allies freed the city of Paris from the Germans.

The Germans were losing the war. But they were not ready to surrender. Then the Allies attacked Germany. Allied planes dropped bombs on German cities. Many cities were destroyed. At last, the Germans knew they could not win. Adolf Hitler killed himself. A few days later, on May 7, 1945, Germany surrendered. The war in Europe had ended.

The world soon learned about the terrible things the Nazis had done during the war. Hitler had planned to kill all Jews as he conquered the world.

Jews and other people in the concentration camps were forced to live in terrible conditions.

Prisoners in a concentration camp in Germany

About six million Jews from all over Europe were killed by Nazis during the war. At least five million other people were also killed. Most were killed in concentration camps. People in the concentration camps were starved, beaten, and forced to work as slaves. Millions were shot or were killed with poison gas. People who spoke out against Hitler were also sent to the concentration camps. This killing of six million Jews and so many other people is now called the **Holocaust**.

World War II was not over. The war against Japan went on after the war in Europe had ended. The Japanese had captured parts of China. They also had captured islands in the Pacific Ocean, including Guam and the Philippines. The Allies fought hard to free Asia from Japan's control. American soldiers were an important part of these battles.

General Douglas MacArthur of the United States led the Allied soldiers in Asia. MacArthur had promised to help the Philippines become free. He kept his promise. He captured the Philippine capital

Douglas MacArthur

American soldiers helped free many Pacific islands from Japanese control.

American soldiers capture the island of Iwo Jima.

in 1945. There were many other battles. Americans and other Allies slowly recaptured islands from the Japanese.

In 1945 the Allies were winning the war against Japan. But Japan would not surrender. The Japanese believed it was better to die than to surrender. Every day more Allied soldiers were killed in the war with the Japanese.

President Roosevelt had died during the war. Harry Truman was the new President of the United States. He decided to use a powerful weapon to force Japan to surrender. This weapon was called the **atomic bomb**. The atomic bomb was much more dangerous than any other weapon ever used.

President Truman warned Japan. He told Japan that the United States would drop an atomic bomb on a Japanese city. He told Japan that it was time to surrender. But Japan refused.

On August 6, 1945, an American plane dropped an atomic bomb on Hiroshima, a Japanese city. Thousands of people were killed. Most of the city was destroyed. But Japan would not surrender. Three days later, Americans dropped an atomic bomb on the Japanese city of Nagasaki. This time, the Japanese surrendered. There was peace in the world again.

World War II caused the deaths of millions of people. Many cities and roads were destroyed. Many Europeans and Asians were starving and homeless.

Harry S. Truman

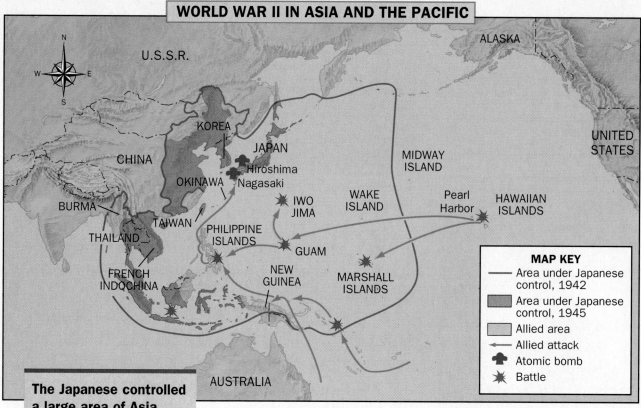

WORLD WAR II IN ASIA AND THE PACIFIC

ALASKA

U.S.S.R.

KOREA

JAPAN

CHINA

Hiroshima
Nagasaki

OKINAWA

MIDWAY
ISLAND

UNITED
STATES

BURMA

TAIWAN

IWO
JIMA

WAKE
ISLAND

Pearl
Harbor

HAWAIIAN
ISLANDS

THAILAND

PHILIPPINE
ISLANDS

GUAM

FRENCH
INDOCHINA

NEW
GUINEA

MARSHALL
ISLANDS

MAP KEY
— Area under Japanese control, 1942
▮ Area under Japanese control, 1945
▯ Allied area
← Allied attack
♣ Atomic bomb
✳ Battle

AUSTRALIA

The Japanese controlled a large area of Asia and the Pacific before World War II ended. Was Midway Island under Japanese control?

Powerful nations like Japan and Germany were now weak. Communist nations began in Eastern Europe. After the war, the United States and the Soviet Union were the two strongest world powers. A lot of tension between these two powerful nations would soon lead to a different type of war.

After World War I, Americans did not want to be involved in the problems of other countries. They did not want to fight in another war. This **isolationism** ended when the United States entered World War II. After World War II, the United States did not return to isolationism. Instead, Americans helped their allies become stronger. The United States worked to spread democracy in nations such as Japan and Italy. The United States also helped **rebuild** many nations in Europe.

People around the world decided it was time to work for peace. They did not want another world war. In the next chapter, you will learn how nations worked together for peace.

The sky after an atomic bomb landed on Nagasaki

Anne Frank (1929–1945)

Anne Frank was a Jewish girl who lived during World War II. She and her family hid from the Nazis during the Holocaust. The diary that Anne wrote while in hiding tells what life was like for many Jews during this terrible time.

Anne Frank was born in Frankfurt, Germany, in 1929. Anne and her mother, father, and sister moved to Holland in 1933. They moved when the Nazis began to take away the rights of Jewish Germans.

In 1942 the Nazis took control of Holland. To hide from the Nazis, Anne's family began living in a secret place behind the office of her father's business. Four other Jewish people hid with the Franks. They all had to be very quiet so that they would not be discovered. Sometimes they would have to sit for hours without moving. They could not turn on lights at night. Friends who were not Jewish would sneak food, clothing, and books to the families.

While in hiding, Anne Frank wrote her thoughts in a diary. She described what it was like to live in hiding. She wrote about her hopes for the future.

Two years later the Nazis discovered the secret hiding place. The Franks and the other Jewish people were sent to concentration camps. Anne died in a camp when she was 15 years old.

After World War II ended, people were looking through the ruins of the office building where Anne had hid. There they found Anne's diary. In 1947 her diary was made into a book called *The Diary of a Young Girl*. It was also made into a movie.

Anne's diary is famous throughout the world. Today the place where Anne and her family hid is the Anne Frank Museum. Near the museum is a statue that honors the memory of Anne Frank.

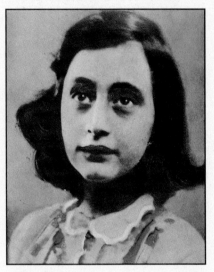

Anne Frank

Building where Anne Frank and her family hid

Using Vocabulary

Finish the Paragraph   Use the words in dark print to finish the paragraph below. Write on the correct blank lines the words you choose.

rebuild   D-Day   atomic bomb   isolationism

Before World War II, Americans did not want to be involved with the

problems of other nations. This was called _____. But after

Japan attacked Pearl Harbor, the United States entered the war. On June 6,

1944, or _____, American soldiers and Allied soldiers landed in

France. They conquered Germany by 1945. To force Japan to surrender, the

United States dropped a deadly weapon called the _____ on two

Japanese cities. After the war, Americans helped _____ many

European cities and towns that had been destroyed.

Read and Remember

Finish Up   Choose words in dark print to best complete the sentences. Write the words on the correct blank lines.

**Anne Frank   concentration   Hitler
Eisenhower   world powers**

1. _____ led the Allied soldiers to free France from Germany.

2. _____ planned to kill all Jews as he conquered the world.

3. Millions of Jews were killed in _____ camps during the Holocaust.

4. _____ wrote a diary about her life during the Holocaust.

5. After World War II, the United States and the Soviet Union were the two

   strongest _____ .

Think and Apply

Distinguishing Relevant Information   Information that is **relevant** is information that is important for what you want to say or write. Imagine that you want to tell a friend about World War II in the Pacific. Read each sentence below. Decide which sentences are relevant to what you will say. Put a check (✔) next to the relevant sentences. There are three relevant sentences.

_____ **1.** The Allies went to Africa to fight Germany and Italy.

_____ **2.** The Japanese captured many islands in the Pacific Ocean.

_____ **3.** On D-Day the Allies began their fight to free France.

_____ **4.** General Douglas MacArthur led the Allied soldiers to free the Philippines.

_____ **5.** American planes dropped atomic bombs on Hiroshima and Nagasaki.

Skill Builder

Reading a Time Line   Dates tell us when events in history happened. A **time line** helps us show which events happened first. Look at the time line below. Then write the answer to each question.

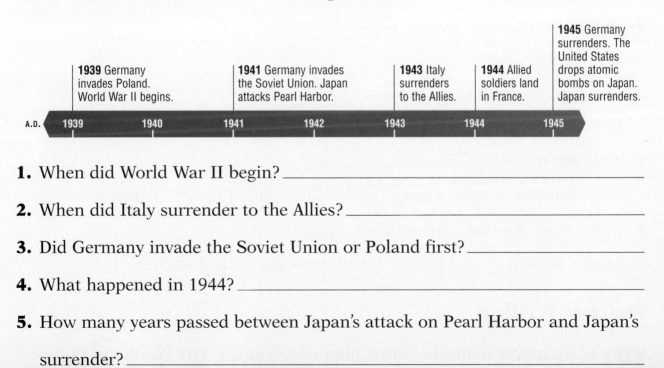

1. When did World War II begin? _____

2. When did Italy surrender to the Allies? _____

3. Did Germany invade the Soviet Union or Poland first? _____

4. What happened in 1944? _____

5. How many years passed between Japan's attack on Pearl Harbor and Japan's

   surrender? _____

83

Reading a Flow Chart A **flow chart** is a chart that shows you facts in the correct order they occur. The flow chart on this page shows how **sonar** was sometimes used to destroy submarines in World War II. Sonar is a type of technology that can allow ships to locate objects underwater. Ships send **sound waves** that bounce off of an object that is in the path of the waves. Read the flow chart. Then circle the words that best complete the sentences.

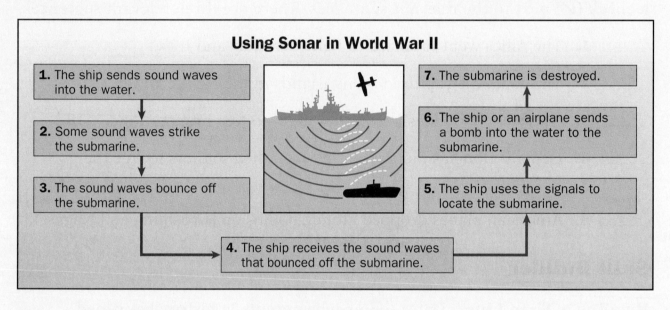

Using Sonar in World War II

1. The ship sends sound waves into the water.

2. Some sound waves strike the submarine.

3. The sound waves bounce off the submarine.

4. The ship receives the sound waves that bounced off the submarine.

5. The ship uses the signals to locate the submarine.

6. The ship or an airplane sends a bomb into the water to the submarine.

7. The submarine is destroyed.

1. In the first step, the _____ sends sound waves into the water.

  submarine   airplane   ship

2. In Step 3, the _____ bounce off the submarine.

  sound waves   bombs   fish

3. The ship receives the sound waves in _____ .

  Step 2   Step 4   Step 6

4. After the ship locates the submarine, it _____ .

  sends a bomb into the water   sends more sound waves   flees

5. In the final step, the submarine _____ .

  bombs the ship   goes to the top of the water   is destroyed

Journal Writing

Write a paragraph about the Allies' plan to defeat the Axis Powers in Europe.

CHAPTER

11

The United Nations

After World War I, many nations worked together for world peace. They were part of the **organization** called the League of Nations. But the League of Nations was weak. It could not prevent World War II from starting. During World War II, the Allies decided to start a new organization that would work for peace. This organization is called the **United Nations**.

Why did the League of Nations fail? One reason was that it did not have its own army. It was also weak because important world powers were not members. The United States was not a member. The Soviet Union, Germany, Italy, and Japan all left the League before World War II. Without strong members and an army, the League could not stop wars between nations. The League of Nations finally ended in 1946.

THINK ABOUT AS YOU READ

1. Why was the United Nations formed?
2. What are the parts of the United Nations?
3. How has the United Nations helped keep peace?

NEW WORDS

♦ organization
♦ United Nations
♦ General Assembly
♦ delegates
♦ secretary-general
♦ Security Council
♦ permanent
♦ resolutions
♦ vetoes
♦ Persian Gulf War

PEOPLE & PLACES

♦ New York City
♦ Iraq
♦ Kuwait
♦ Jean-Bertrand Aristide
♦ Somalia
♦ Bosnia and Herzegovina

The United Nations was formed in 1945. This meeting in 1995 marked fifty years that the UN has worked for world peace.

The United Nations building in New York City

The UN flag

The UN Security Council

The United Nations, or UN, was formed in 1945. It began with 51 members. Today 185 nations are members of the UN. The UN headquarters are in New York City in the United States.

The UN sometimes sends soldiers to other nations to work for peace. It also gives food and medicine to millions of people in needy nations. The UN teaches people new ways to grow more food. Teachers from the UN help needy people learn to read and write.

The United Nations has many parts. One part is the **General Assembly**. Every member nation of the UN sends **delegates** to the General Assembly. Each member nation has one vote. The General Assembly meets every year. The leader of the United Nations is called the **secretary-general**. Every five years the General Assembly chooses a new secretary-general.

The **Security Council** is the most powerful part of the UN. The Security Council has 15 member nations. There are five **permanent** members. The United States, Great Britain, France, Russia, and China are the five permanent members. Ten other members are chosen by the General Assembly. They work on the Security Council for two years.

The members of the Security Council vote on actions that the United Nations can take to keep peace. They also vote on other **resolutions** that tell what they think of the actions of some nations. All five permanent members of the Security Council must agree on the resolution. If a permanent member **vetoes** a resolution, the resolution is not passed. The General Assembly can also vote on resolutions. Two thirds of the General Assembly must agree in order for the resolution to pass.

The Security Council can send UN soldiers to a land where there is fighting. These soldiers come from many nations. They try to stop nations from fighting. They do not fight to win a war. They try to win peace.

The UN sent soldiers to Bosnia and Herzegovina to try to help end the civil war there.

UN soldier during the Persian Gulf War

The UN hoped to bring peace and food to the people of Somalia.

In 1990 the oil-rich nation Iraq attacked its neighbor Kuwait. Iraq wanted Kuwait's oil wells. The UN demanded that Iraq leave Kuwait. The United States and many other UN nations sent soldiers to help Kuwait become free. In 1991 a short war was fought. It was called the **Persian Gulf War**. Iraq lost the war, and Kuwait was freed. Many people were glad that the UN was able to help. It had stopped one country from taking over another country.

The UN also helped Haiti. The people of Haiti had elected Jean-Bertrand Aristide as president. But in 1991 the military leader of Haiti used force to take control of Haiti away from Aristide. In 1994 the UN voted to send soldiers to Haiti. Within months, Aristide was again the leader of Haiti.

Many times the UN has not been able to stop wars in countries. In 1992 the UN sent a peace-keeping force to try to end a civil war in the African country of Somalia. The UN also hoped to feed the starving people in the country. The UN saved many people, but it was not able to end the civil war.

In 1992 a civil war began in the European nation of Bosnia and Herzegovina. The UN sent soldiers there to work for peace. But the fighting continued. In November 1995, the United States worked with the Bosnian groups to create a peace treaty. There is still serious tension in this nation, but the UN continues its peace-keeping efforts.

Using Vocabulary

Find the Meaning   Write on the blank the word or words that best complete each sentence.

1. The **United Nations** is an organization of nations that works for

_____ .

world trade   world peace   world banks

2. **Delegates** in the United Nations are people who _____ member nations.

represent   trust   are at war with

3. The **secretary-general** is the leader of the _____ .

League of Nations   country of Somalia   United Nations

4. A **permanent** member of the Security Council is a member

_____ .

for two years   for five years   every year

Read and Remember

Find the Answer   Put a check (✔) next to each sentence that tells something true about the United Nations. You should check five sentences.

_____ **1.** The United Nations was formed in 1945.

_____ **2.** Every member nation of the UN is part of the General Assembly.

_____ **3.** The Security Council can never send soldiers to nations where there is fighting.

_____ **4.** The UN helped put President Aristide back in power in Haiti.

_____ **5.** The UN teaches people new ways to grow more food.

_____ **6.** The UN has always been able to stop wars in different parts of the world.

_____ **7.** A vote against a resolution is called an organization.

_____ **8.** The UN is working for peace in Bosnia and Herzegovina.

Skill Builder

Reading a Diagram A **diagram** is a way of showing information. Study the diagram below of the headquarters of the United Nations. Then write a sentence to answer each question.

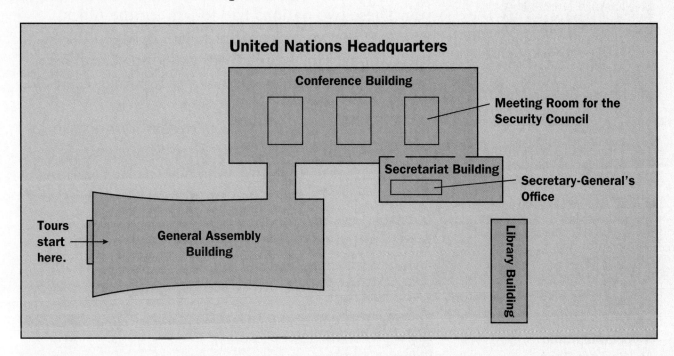

1. What four buildings of the UN headquarters are shown in the diagram?

_____

_____

2. In what building does the Security Council meet?_____

_____

3. To what building would you go to get a tour of the UN headquarters?

_____

4. In what building is the secretary-general's office?_____

_____

CHAPTER 12

The Cold War

NEW WORDS

- ◆ **conflict**
- ◆ **Cold War**
- ◆ **resist**
- ◆ **Marshall Plan**
- ◆ **North Atlantic Treaty Organization**
- ◆ **Warsaw Pact**
- ◆ **nuclear arms race**
- ◆ **missiles**
- ◆ **space race**
- ◆ **satellite**
- ◆ **Korean War**
- ◆ **nuclear war**

PEOPLE & PLACES

- ◆ **Korea**
- ◆ **Berlin**
- ◆ **Cuba**
- ◆ **John F. Kennedy**

When World War II ended, many nations that had fought in the war were very weak. But the United States and the Soviet Union were stronger than they had been before the war. These two nations had fought for the Allies. But after the war, a **conflict** began between the two nations. This conflict was called the **Cold War** because there was usually not any fighting. The Cold War was mostly fought with angry words.

The Cold War was a war between Communists and non-Communists. The United States and its allies wanted to spread democracy to other nations. The Soviet Union and its Communist allies wanted to spread communism. There was much tension between the two sides. The Communists and the non-Communists did not trust one another. People were afraid that a third world war might occur.

The Soviet Union built the Berlin Wall to keep East Germans from escaping into West Berlin.

The Soviet Union wanted to have a strong control over Eastern Europe. After World War II ended, the Soviet Union forced many Eastern European nations to have Communist governments. Some of these nations were Czechoslovakia, Poland, Hungary, and part of Germany. Winston Churchill said that an "Iron Curtain" had come down over Eastern Europe. The Soviet Union was the leading power behind the Iron Curtain.

The Marshall Plan helped rebuild the nations of Western Europe.

In 1947 the United States said that it would help nations **resist** the spread of communism. One way it did this was with the **Marshall Plan** in 1948. This plan allowed the United States to send money to help rebuild Western Europe. The Marshall Plan helped nations in Western Europe become stronger. Communism did not spread to Western Europe.

In 1949 the United States, Canada, and many Western European nations started a new military organization. This was the **North Atlantic Treaty Organization,** or NATO. The NATO nations agreed to help protect one another from the Soviet Union and other Communist nations. Soldiers from member nations work for NATO. Today there are 16 nations that belong to NATO.

In 1955 the Soviet Union and other Eastern European nations signed a treaty called the **Warsaw Pact**. Like NATO, the Warsaw Pact nations agreed to help one another if any of them was attacked.

The Cold War led to many changes. One change was new technology. During World War II, the United States was the only country that built an atomic bomb. By 1949 the Soviets had their own atomic bomb. This was the beginning of the **nuclear arms race**. The United States and the Soviet Union began testing other types of nuclear weapons. They also began to build powerful new weapons called **missiles**.

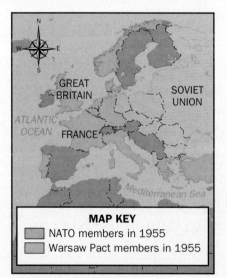

MAP KEY
NATO members in 1955
Warsaw Pact members in 1955

Nations of NATO and the Warsaw Pact in 1955

The Cold War also led to the **space race**. In 1957 the Soviet Union sent its first **satellite** into space.

The Cold War led to a space race between the Soviet Union and the United States. In 1969 Americans walked on the moon.

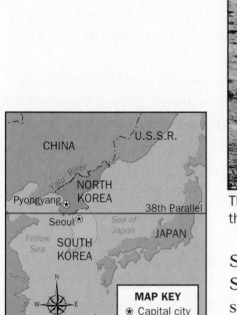

North Korea and South Korea

UN soldier in Korea

Satellites are machines that travel around Earth. Soon after that, the United States began its own space program. In 1961 the Soviets sent a man into space. In 1969 the United States sent the first people to the moon. Both nations continued to spend a lot of money on their space programs.

The Cold War led to a real war in Korea, a country in eastern Asia. After World War II, the Soviet Union had soldiers in northern Korea. The United States had soldiers in southern Korea. When all the soldiers left, Korea was divided into two parts. North Korea became a Communist state. In 1950 the Communists invaded South Korea. They wanted to make Korea one Communist nation.

The United States did not want South Korea to be a Communist nation. The United States and the United Nations sent soldiers to fight in the **Korean War**. For three years they helped the South Koreans fight the North Koreans. The Communists were forced back into North Korea. At last the fighting ended. North Korea and South Korea are two separate nations today.

Cuba

John F. Kennedy

American missiles being tested

The Cold War also took place in Germany. After World War II, Germany was divided into four parts. In 1949 three parts became West Germany. West Germany was a democracy. The fourth part became East Germany. East Germany had a Communist government controlled by the Soviet Union. The capital city of Berlin was also divided. There was much more freedom in West Berlin. The standard of living there was much higher than in East Berlin. Many people from East Germany tried to escape to West Berlin.

In 1961 the Soviets built a wall between East Berlin and West Berlin. They built the wall in order to stop East Germans from escaping into West Berlin. The United States wanted the Soviets to tear down the Berlin Wall. But the wall was not removed for many years.

The Cold War also spread to Cuba. Cuba is an island near Florida. It became a Communist nation in 1961. In 1962 the Soviet Union sent missiles to Cuba. Many people thought these missiles might be used to destroy American cities. John F. Kennedy was the President of the United States. He demanded that the Soviets remove the missiles. People were afraid that a **nuclear war** might occur. After a few days, the Soviets removed the missiles from Cuba.

The Cold War lasted more than forty years. During that time, the United States and the Soviet Union tried to remove some of the tension between the two nations. One way they did that was by limiting nuclear weapons during the 1970s and 1980s.

There are still Communist nations in the world today. But people in Eastern Europe did not like communism. After many years, communism in Eastern Europe became weaker. By the year 1991 communism in Eastern Europe and the Soviet Union had ended. This brought an end to the Cold War. You will learn about these changes in Chapter 19.

Using Vocabulary

Finish Up Choose the word or words in dark print to best complete each sentence. Write the word or words on the correct blank line.

nuclear war   Cold War   NATO   Marshall Plan

1. The conflict between Communist nations and non-Communist nations was

called the _____.

2. The _____ allowed the United States to send money to help rebuild Western Europe.

3. The organization that worked to prevent the spread of communism was called

_____.

4. A _____ is a war that uses such weapons as the atomic bomb.

Read and Remember

Finish the Sentence Draw a circle around the word or words that best complete each sentence.

1. At the end of World War II, the United States and the Soviet Union were _____ than other nations.

stronger   weaker   slower

2. The United States created the Marshall Plan to help European nations _____ the spread of communism.

enjoy   encourage   resist

3. The Soviet Union forced Czechoslovakia and _____ to have Communist governments.

China   Poland   West Germany

4. The United States sent people to the moon because of the _____.

nuclear arms race   space race   Korean War

5. In 1950 Communists invaded _____.

Cuba   North Korea   South Korea

6. Cuba became a _____ in 1961.

Communist nation   democracy   republic

Think and Apply

Understanding Different Points of View   People can look in different ways at something that happens. Look at these two points of view about World War II.

World War II was a war that never should have been fought.
World War II was important because it ended the Holocaust.

The Soviet Union and the United States had different points of view during the Cold War. Read each sentence below. Write **Soviet** next to the sentences that might show the point of view of a Soviet during the Cold War. Write **American** next to the sentences that might show the point of view of an American during the Cold War.

_____ **1.** Germany, Italy, and Japan should be democracies.

_____ **2.** Eastern European countries should have Communist governments.

_____ **3.** East Germans should not go to West Berlin.

_____ **4.** The Berlin Wall should be removed.

_____ **5.** Korea should be one Communist nation.

_____ **6.** The United Nations should send soldiers to South Korea to fight the North Koreans.

_____ **7.** It is important to stop the spread of communism and to help nations become democracies.

_____ **8.** Cuba should have powerful missiles.

Crossword Puzzle

Each sentence below has a word missing. Choose the missing word for each sentence from the words in dark print. Then write the words in the correct places on the puzzle.

────────────────── **ACROSS** ──────────────────

NATO   Communist   arms   Iron

1. Churchill said that an "_____ Curtain" had come down over Eastern Europe.

2. The Warsaw Pact was signed by the _____ nations of Eastern Europe.

3. The United States and Canada are members of _____.

4. The United States and the Soviet Union began a nuclear _____ race.

────────────────── **DOWN** ──────────────────

nuclear   missiles   Berlin   control

5. Many people from East Germany tried to escape to West _____.

6. The Soviet Union wanted to _____ the nations of Eastern Europe.

7. The atomic bomb is a _____ weapon.

8. John F. Kennedy told the Soviet Union to remove its _____ from Cuba.

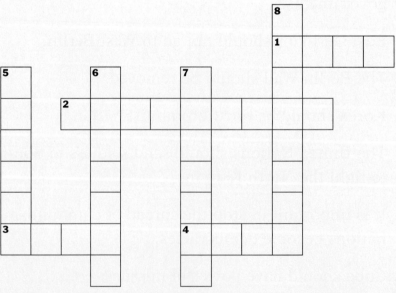

CHAPTER 13

China Becomes a Communist Nation

THINK ABOUT AS YOU READ

1. How did China become a Communist nation?
2. Why did China have civil wars?
3. What is China like today?

NEW WORDS

♦ warlords
♦ better relations
♦ protesters
♦ Cultural Revolution
♦ recover

PEOPLE & PLACES

♦ Nationalists
♦ Sun Yat-sen
♦ Chiang Kai-shek
♦ Mao Zedong
♦ Taiwan
♦ People's Republic of China
♦ Deng Xiaoping
♦ Jiang Zemin
♦ Red Guards

China was an empire for more than 2,000 years. However, during the 1800s China's trade and some of its land were controlled by imperialist nations. Many Chinese wanted China to become an industrial nation. They did not want China to be controlled by emperors or other nations. Nationalism became very important.

A group of people called Nationalists wanted to change the government of China. A man named Sun Yat-sen was the leader of the Nationalists. In 1911 he helped China become a republic. China no longer had an emperor.

Sun Yat-sen became the president of the new republic. He hoped that all of China would become a democracy. But the new government was weak. Different **warlords** ruled small parts of China. A civil war began between the Nationalists and China's warlords.

China today is still a strong Communist nation.

Sun Yat-sen

Chiang Kai-shek

Communist soldiers marching through a Chinese city in 1949

When World War I began, the Chinese joined the Allies against the Central Powers. But after the war, China's civil war continued. Sun Yat-sen asked the Soviet Union to help the Nationalists fight. The Soviet Union agreed to help teach the Nationalist army how to fight. Some Chinese people liked the Communist ideas of the Soviet Union. They started a Communist party. The Communists worked with the Nationalists to fight the warlords.

Sun Yat-sen died during the civil war in China. A man named Chiang Kai-shek became the new leader of the Nationalists. The Nationalists and the Communists continued the fight against the warlords. But Chiang Kai-shek did not trust the Communists. He thought that the Soviet Union wanted the Communists to rule China after the warlords were defeated. Chiang started a battle against the Communists. Most of the Communists were killed. The rest of the Communists hid from the Nationalists.

By 1928 China was united and ruled by the Nationalists. Chiang Kai-shek promised democracy and new rights for the Chinese. But Chiang did not give people all the freedom he had promised. Life did not improve for the millions of poor peasants. Many peasants decided to become Communists. One of these peasants was Mao Zedong. Mao started a Communist army.

Mao led the Communists in another civil war in 1930. This time the Nationalists pushed the Communists into the northwest part of China.

In 1937 Japan attacked China. Japan knew that the Chinese were fighting a civil war. The Japanese decided that it was a good time to attack China. The Chinese Communists and the Chinese Nationalists fought together against the Japanese. The Japanese conquered much of China. But the Chinese did not stop fighting. When Japan lost World War II, all of China became free of Japanese control.

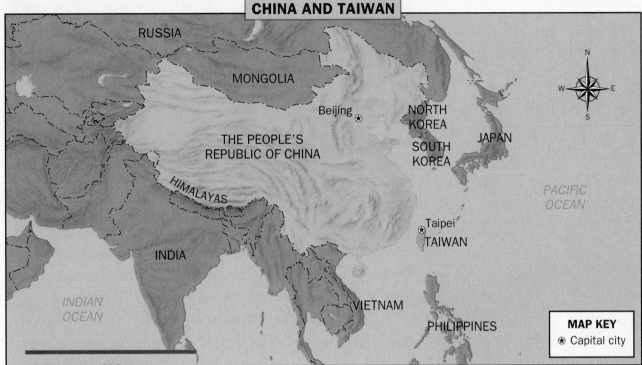

RUSSIA

MONGOLIA

Beijing ⊛

THE PEOPLE'S
REPUBLIC OF CHINA

NORTH
KOREA

SOUTH
KOREA

JAPAN

HIMALAYAS

PACIFIC
OCEAN

INDIA

Taipei
⊛
TAIWAN

INDIAN
OCEAN

VIETNAM

PHILIPPINES

MAP KEY
⊛ Capital city

When the Chinese
Communists defeated
the Nationalists in
1949, the Nationalists
fled to the island of
Taiwan. What is the
capital of Taiwan?

Mao Zedong

After World War II, the Nationalists and the
Communists in China fought again. In 1949
the Communists won. Chiang Kai-shek and the
Nationalists escaped to an island near China. This
island is called Taiwan.

Since 1949 Communists have ruled China. They
changed its name to the People's Republic of China.
More than one billion people live in China under the
Communist government. The Nationalists rule
Taiwan. Taiwan is not a Communist nation.

Mao Zedong ruled the People's Republic of China
until he died in 1976. He was a dictator. Everyone
had to obey Mao. There was no freedom. People who
spoke out against Mao were sent to jail or killed.
All businesses were owned by the government. But
Mao also helped China become a world power. The
Chinese had a strong army. They learned how to
build atomic bombs.

For many years, the United States and China
were enemies. This was a result of the Cold War. The
United States did not want China to be a Communist
nation. Since 1972 there have been **better relations**

In 1989 many Chinese gathered in cities and spoke out against communism. Many of these protesters were killed by soldiers.

Deng Xiaoping

Woman in Beijing

between the nations. American Presidents have visited China. The two nations trade with each other. Many Americans have businesses in China.

A few years after Mao died, a man named Deng Xiaoping became the leader of China's government. He helped China become a stronger nation. Deng increased China's trade with other countries. He also helped the growth of business in China. He allowed Chinese people to own some farms and businesses. Many Chinese earned more money.

Many Chinese wanted Deng to bring democracy to China. In 1989 Chinese university students tried to win more freedom. They became **protesters**. They marched in the streets of Beijing and other cities. The students carried signs that said that China needed freedom and democracy.

Deng Xiaoping did not want China to become a democracy. He sent the Chinese army to fight the protesters. Thousands of protesters were killed by the army. The protests ended. There was even less freedom in China after the protests ended.

Since 1911 China has changed from a nation ruled by emperors to a Communist nation. China is a world power today. Jiang Zemin is now China's leader. More people own businesses. Most Chinese have enough food and can read and write. But there is not much freedom in China today. Many people still hope that China will become a democracy.

Mao Zedong (1893–1976)

Mao Zedong led the fight to make China a strong Communist nation. He was one of the most powerful leaders in China's history.

Mao was born to a poor family in China in 1893. He became interested in communism while he was working in Beijing. Mao led peasants to form the Chinese Communist party in 1921. In 1949 the Communists defeated the Nationalists. Mao became the leader of the People's Republic of China.

Mao Zedong

Mao was a dictator. He controlled every part of the daily lives of the Chinese. He had pictures of himself put on posters all over China. The Chinese had to study Mao's ideas. The government took control of farms and businesses. Most people worked on collective farms. People were paid very low wages.

Some Chinese leaders tried to help China become a more modern nation. But Mao said that these changes went against the ideas of communism. In 1966 Mao began the **Cultural Revolution** to make communism in China stronger. He sent soldiers called the Red Guards all over China. The Red Guards closed schools and colleges. Scientists, factory owners, doctors, and other people were sent to work on farms. Many people were killed or arrested. The revolution led to years of hard times in China. Factories closed. Farmers grew less food.

Red Guards during the Cultural Revolution

Mao realized that China was in trouble. He made efforts to help China **recover**. Schools opened again. People went back to work. But it was hard to bring back order to China.

Mao died in 1976. He left behind a China that was struggling with many problems. But Mao died believing in communism. Even today his writings are studied by people in other nations.

Using Vocabulary

Match Up Finish the sentences in Group A with words from Group B. Write the letter of each correct answer on the blank line.

Group A

1. Chinese _____ were people who ruled small parts of China.

2. People who speak out against an issue or a government are _____ .

3. One example of _____ between the United States and China is an increase of trade.

★ **4.** The _____ was a time in which the Red Guards closed schools and sent people to work on farms.

Group B

a. protesters

b. warlords

c. Cultural Revolution

d. better relations

Read and Remember

Write the Answer Write one or more sentences to answer each question.

1. Why did Chiang Kai-shek order the Nationalists to fight the Communists?

_____

2. Why did Japan think 1937 was a good time to attack China? _____

_____

3. In what ways did Deng Xiaoping help China become a stronger nation?

_____

_____

★ **4.** In what ways was Mao Zedong a dictator? _____

_____

Think and Apply

Sequencing Events Write the numbers **1, 2, 3, 4,** and **5** next to these sentences to show the correct order. The first one is done for you.

_____ China and the United States began to trade with each other after 1972.

_____ Chiang Kai-shek started a battle against the Communists in China.

__1__ Sun Yat-sen became the leader of the Nationalists.

_____ Mao Zedong led the Communists to gain control of China in 1949.

_____ Deng Xiaoping sent the army to fight protesters in Beijing.

Skill Builder

Reading a Chart Read the chart below. Then write the answer to each question.

LEADERS OF CHINA

Leader	When did he become leader?	Communist or Nationalist?	What did he do?
Sun Yat-sen	1911	Nationalist	Helped China become a republic.
Chiang Kai-shek	1926	Nationalist	Defeated the warlords in China. Became president of Taiwan in 1949.
Mao Zedong	1949	Communist	Helped China become a Communist nation. Started a cultural revolution.
Deng Xiaoping	1980	Communist	Helped the growth of business in China.

1. Which two leaders were Nationalists? _____

2. When did Mao become China's leader? _____

3. Who became president of Taiwan in 1949? _____

4. Who helped China become a republic? _____

5. What did Deng Xiaoping do for China? _____

_____

CHAPTER 14

The Vietnam War

THINK ABOUT AS YOU READ

1. Why did wars begin in Southeast Asia?
2. Why did the United States fight in the Vietnam War?
3. How have the United States and Vietnam improved relations?

NEW WORDS

♦ Vietnam War
♦ troops
♦ civilians
♦ protested
♦ cease-fire
♦ damage
♦ refugees
♦ boat people

PEOPLE & PLACES

♦ Southeast Asia
♦ Vietnam
♦ North Vietnam
♦ South Vietnam
♦ Viet Cong
♦ Ho Chi Minh
♦ Australia
♦ New Zealand
♦ Thailand
♦ Cambodia
♦ Laos

You have read how in the 1950s the Korean War brought fighting to the Cold War. It turned the Cold War into a hot war. In 1957 fighting began that turned the Cold War into a hot war again. This was the **Vietnam War**. The Vietnam War took place in Southeast Asia.

Southeast Asia separates the Indian Ocean and the Pacific Ocean. Part of Southeast Asia is a large peninsula that is south of China. The rest of the region is made up of thousands of islands. There are forests, rivers, fertile soil, and a lot of rain. Southeast Asia is rich in natural resources.

Vietnam is a country in Southeast Asia. It was a French colony for many years. Vietnam won its independence from France in 1954. Then Vietnam was divided into two countries called North Vietnam and South Vietnam. A Communist government was

Battles of the Vietnam War often were fought in the jungle.

North Vietnamese soldiers helped the Viet Cong fight against the South Vietnamese government.

The Vietnam War

Ho Chi Minh

set up in North Vietnam. South Vietnam was a non-Communist republic.

Many Communists lived in South Vietnam. They were called the Viet Cong. The Viet Cong wanted South Vietnam to be a Communist nation. In 1957 the Viet Cong began to fight against the South Vietnamese government.

North Vietnam wanted South Vietnam to have a Communist government, too. A man named Ho Chi Minh was the president of North Vietnam. He sent soldiers and weapons to help the Viet Cong. The Soviet Union and China also helped the Viet Cong.

The United States wanted to stop the spread of communism in Southeast Asia. So it helped the government of South Vietnam. At first, the United States just sent money and weapons to South Vietnam. Then it began to send soldiers to help teach the South Vietnamese how to fight. Other countries also helped South Vietnam. These countries were Australia, New Zealand, South Korea, Thailand, and the Philippines.

By 1965 the fighting had spread to two countries that shared Vietnam's western border. These two

American soldiers walking in a rice field in South Vietnam

Many helicopters were used during the Vietnam War.

Americans protesting against the Vietnam War

countries were Cambodia and Laos. Then the United States became more involved in the war. American planes dropped bombs on North Vietnam. The United States also sent thousands of American **troops** to help South Vietnam. By 1969 there were over 500,000 soldiers from the United States that were involved in the Vietnam War.

For a long time, neither side was winning the war. The United States had a lot of modern technology and weapons. But the Viet Cong and the North Vietnamese knew the land of Vietnam. They fought well in the jungles and mountains of Vietnam. The Viet Cong also attacked many villages in South Vietnam. Millions of soldiers and **civilians** died during the Vietnam War. Civilians are people that are not in the military.

Many Americans did not think that the United States should fight in Vietnam. They said that too many Americans were dying in the war. They believed that too much money was being spent on the war. These Americans **protested** against the Vietnam War. In many cities large numbers of people marched to show that they were against the war. Some people burned American flags.

In 1973 the United States, South Vietnam, North Vietnam, and the Viet Cong signed a **cease-fire** agreement. This means that they agreed to stop fighting. American troops came home.

Fighting began again soon after the American troops left. By 1975 North Vietnam and the Viet Cong had defeated South Vietnam. In 1976 North Vietnam and South Vietnam became one nation called Vietnam. Vietnam became a Communist nation. Laos and Cambodia also became Communist nations. The Communist governments took over businesses and farms. Many people were executed by the Communists.

More than 2 million people from Vietnam were killed during the war. Much of North Vietnam was

Many refugees traveled by boat to reach safe countries. These boat people are arriving in Hong Kong near China.

American soldiers captured during the Vietnam War

People in Vietnam

destroyed. Large parts of Laos and Cambodia were also destroyed. Most of the fighting had taken place in South Vietnam. So South Vietnam had the most **damage** to its villages, cities, and roads.

About half of South Vietnam's population became **refugees**. Refugees are people who leave their country in order to escape danger. By the early 1980s, millions of refugees had left Vietnam, Cambodia, and Laos. Some refugees lived in camps near Thailand's border with Laos and Cambodia. Other people became **boat people**. These refugees escaped from their countries in boats. They hoped to reach safe countries or to be rescued. Many of the boat people moved to other parts of Asia. The largest number of boat people came to the United States.

Many people in the United States and in Vietnam still feel angry about the Vietnam War. But the nations are looking to the future. In recent years the United States and Vietnam have worked to improve relations. The government of Vietnam has helped to find and return the bodies of American soldiers who were killed in Vietnam. In 1995 the United States agreed to trade with Vietnam. These better relations give people hope that peace will continue.

Using Vocabulary

Finish the Paragraph   Use the words in dark print to finish the paragraph below. Write on the correct blank lines the words you choose.

refugees   boat people   cease-fire   damage

There was much fighting during the Vietnam War. South Vietnam received

the most _____, because more roads, buildings, and farms were

destroyed there than in North Vietnam. The United States, South Vietnam, and

North Vietnam agreed to stop fighting when they signed a _____

agreement. But North Vietnam later gained control of South Vietnam. More

than half of South Vietnam's population became _____ because

they wanted to escape danger in their country. Some of these people became

_____ who tried to reach safe countries by traveling on water.

Read and Remember

Choose the Answer   Draw a circle around the correct answer.

1. Who started a war against the South Vietnamese government in 1957?

the Soviets   the Viet Cong   South Koreans

2. Why did the United States help South Vietnam in the war?

to increase trade   to gain land   to stop the spread of communism

3. Where else did fighting occur during the Vietnam War?

Canada and Mexico   Cambodia and Laos   France and China

4. What kind of government was set up in Vietnam after the war?

Communist government   democracy   monarchy

5. What did many Americans do to protest the Vietnam War?

became soldiers   held marches   sent money to South Vietnam

Skill Builder

Reading a Resource Map   A **resource map** uses symbols to show where different natural resources are found. The map key tells you what each symbol means. Southeast Asia has many natural resources. It has many forests and fish. The resource map below shows where some other natural resources are found in Southeast Asia. Study the map and the map key. Then write the answer to each question.

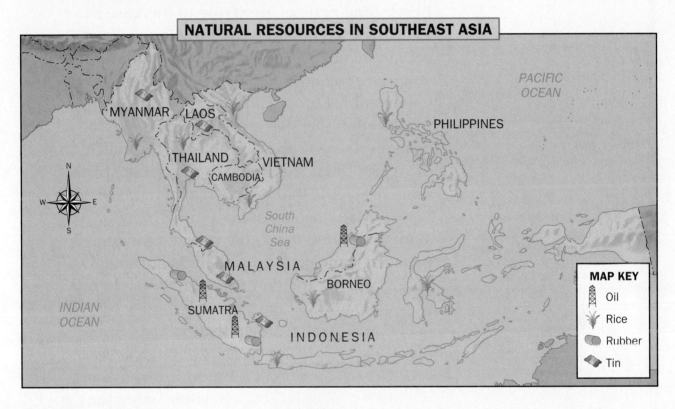

NATURAL RESOURCES IN SOUTHEAST ASIA

MAP KEY
- Oil
- Rice
- Rubber
- Tin

1. What symbol is used to show rubber? _____

2. Does the map show that Laos has tin? _____

3. What is one resource of Vietnam? _____

4. Does the map show that the Philippines has oil? _____

5. Which two countries have both tin and rice? _____

_____

6. Which resource can be found in more places in Southeast Asia than any

other resource? _____

Unit 4   The World Today

The world today is very different from the world before World War II and the Cold War. Most nations today are independent. Many nations are industrial. Developing nations are trying to increase their industries. Populations are growing. In some countries, people are working for more rights and more freedom. Trade has become very important for most nations.

Although there have been many good changes, there are also problems. Nations in the world today are trying to solve some of the same problems that people had before World War II. Many people are poor and hungry. Many people do not know how to read and write. In some countries, there is not much freedom. Some nations do not have enough money to help their people. Some nations have civil wars. Pollution is increasing.

In some ways, the nations of today have not changed. Millions of people follow old traditions. In some nations of the world, religion is as important today as it was long ago. In developing nations, many farmers still grow food the same way farmers did hundreds of years ago.

How have nations changed since World War II and the Cold War? How have they

PACIFIC OCEAN

ATLANTIC OCEAN

PACIFIC OCEAN

INDIAN OCEAN

stayed the same? Who are some of the important leaders of today? As you read Unit 4, think about the ways that nations of the world today are alike and different. Think about the important problems that many nations are working to solve.

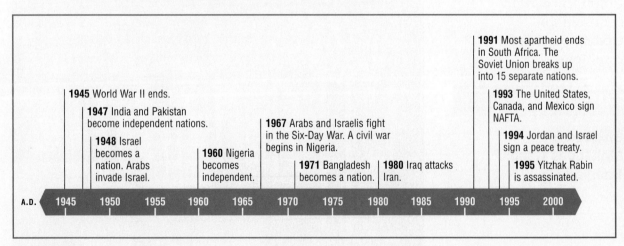

1991 Most apartheid ends in South Africa. The Soviet Union breaks up into 15 separate nations.

1945 World War II ends.

1947 India and Pakistan become independent nations.

1993 The United States, Canada, and Mexico sign NAFTA.

1948 Israel becomes a nation. Arabs invade Israel.

1960 Nigeria becomes independent.

1967 Arabs and Israelis fight in the Six-Day War. A civil war begins in Nigeria.

1994 Jordan and Israel sign a peace treaty.

1971 Bangladesh becomes a nation.

1980 Iraq attacks Iran.

1995 Yitzhak Rabin is assassinated.

A.D. | 1945 | 1950 | 1955 | 1960 | 1965 | 1970 | 1975 | 1980 | 1985 | 1990 | 1995 | 2000

Asia Today

Asia is the world's largest continent. More than half of the world's population is in Asia. The Himalayas, the world's tallest mountains, are in Asia. Long rivers flow through forests and farmland. Deserts cover parts of Asia.

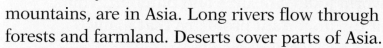

There have been many wars in Asia. You have read how wars were fought in China, Korea, and nations of Southeast Asia. Wars have made it hard for these nations to solve their problems.

Many nations in Asia are **developing nations**. In developing nations, most people earn very little money. The standard of living is low. Hunger and **poverty** are usually large problems. Most people are farmers who work the same way farmers worked long ago. It is hard for them to grow enough food for the people. **Illiteracy** is another problem. Illiteracy

Many Asian cities, such as Hong Kong City, are very large, modern, and crowded.

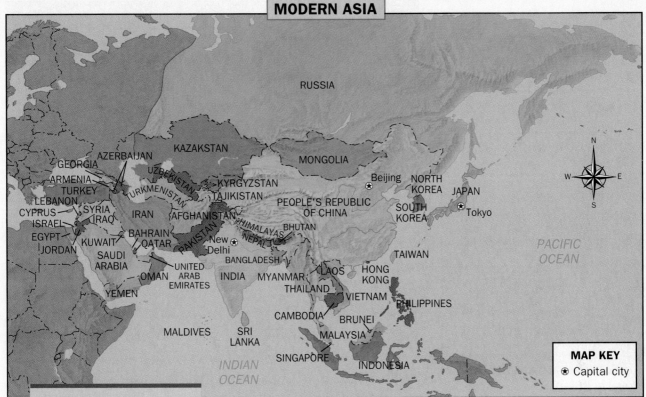

RUSSIA

KAZAKSTAN

MONGOLIA

AZERBAIJAN

GEORGIA

ARMENIA
TURKEY

UZBEKISTAN

KYRGYZSTAN

Beijing ⊛   NORTH
KOREA   JAPAN

TURKMENISTAN
TAJIKISTAN

PEOPLE'S REPUBLIC
OF CHINA

SOUTH
KOREA   ⊛ Tokyo

LEBANON
CYPRUS   SYRIA
ISRAEL   IRAQ   IRAN   AFGHANISTAN

HIMALAYAS   BHUTAN

EGYPT
JORDAN   KUWAIT   BAHRAIN
QATAR   PAKISTAN   New ⊛
Delhi   NEPAL

TAIWAN

PACIFIC
OCEAN

SAUDI
ARABIA   UNITED
ARAB
EMIRATES   OMAN   INDIA   MYANMAR
BANGLADESH   LAOS   HONG
KONG

YEMEN

THAILAND   VIETNAM

PHILIPPINES

CAMBODIA   BRUNEI

MALDIVES   SRI
LANKA   MALAYSIA

SINGAPORE   INDONESIA

INDIAN
OCEAN

MAP KEY
⊛ Capital city

**Asia is the world's
largest continent. Are
nations of the Middle
East part of Asia?**

Worker in a computer factory
in Taiwan

means people cannot read or write. Many developing
nations are trying to build new factories.

Other nations in Asia have become modern
industrial nations. These nations are **developed
nations**. Japan, South Korea, Singapore, and Taiwan
are developed nations. These nations **export** factory
products to many nations. The standard of living is
high in these nations.

Religion is very important in many Asian nations.
Hinduism, Buddhism, Christianity, and Islam are the
main religions in Asia. At times, conflicts about the
religions have caused wars.

India is a large developing nation in southern
Asia. India has more than 936 million people. It is
very crowded. There are not enough schools and
teachers. Less than half of India's people know how
to read. It is hard to grow enough food for all of the
people. But farmers in India are using new ways to
grow more food. Some of these methods come from
the **Green Revolution**. The Green Revolution is a

Mohandas Gandhi helped bring peace and freedom to India.

Poverty in India

A new hotel being built in New Delhi, India's capital

way of farming that uses more irrigation, more energy, and better seeds to grow more crops.

In 1858 India became part of the British empire. Many Indians did not want their country to be ruled by the British. One man, Mohandas Gandhi, helped India become an independent nation again. He said that people should find peaceful ways to end British rule. He told Indians to stop obeying British laws and to stop buying British goods. During the 1920s and 1930s, Gandhi led many peaceful protests against British rule. Millions of Indians took part in the protests. Finally in 1947 India became an independent nation. India became a democracy.

Millions of Muslims lived in India. The Hindus and the Muslims often fought one another about religion. Gandhi tried to end the fighting between the Hindus and the Muslims of India. He helped people to think about how the fighting was hurting India. The leaders of the two religious groups agreed to end the fighting. But in 1948 Mohandas Gandhi was **assassinated** by a Hindu who was angry about the religious problems in India. Since then, Indians have continued to have many riots about religion.

Today India is the world's largest democracy. India is working to become a developed nation. The government is helping farmers use modern methods

Floods in Bangladesh have left millions of people without homes.

Modern rice farming in Japan

to grow food. New factories make cars, clothing, and other products. Each year more schools are built.

In 1947 some of India's Muslims started a new Muslim nation called Pakistan. People in the northeast and northwest parts of India became citizens of Pakistan. The two parts of Pakistan were separated by India. In 1971 the people of eastern Pakistan started their own nation called Bangladesh. Today, Bangladesh and Pakistan are poor, developing nations. Like India, they must solve many problems, including hunger and illiteracy. In 1988 Bangladesh had one of the worst floods in its history. More than 2,000 people were killed. More than 25 million people were left without homes.

Like India, Japan is a very crowded Asian nation. Japan is also a democracy. But unlike India, Japan is a rich, developed nation.

Japan has few natural resources. It does not have much farmland. Only a small part of Japan's people are farmers. They use modern tools and machines on their small farms. They grow a lot of the food Japan needs. The Japanese eat a lot of fish from the sea. Japan must buy some food from other nations.

Most of Japan was destroyed during World War II. After the war, the United States helped Japan rebuild and become a rich democracy. The Japanese built

Supermarket in Japan

Japanese family eating at home

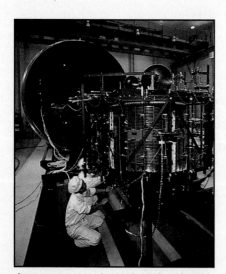
Japanese workers helping build a satellite

Dance and clothing are two traditions in many nations. These two dancers are helping tradition stay important in Indonesia.

thousands of new factories. Today, the Japanese buy raw materials from other nations. They use these raw materials to make cars, televisions, radios, and cameras. Japan sells these products to many nations.

The United States is one of Japan's main **trading partners**. This means that the nations buy products from each other. In recent years, there have been trade problems between the two nations. The United States thinks that Japan should buy many more American products than it already does. Japan thinks it buys enough products from the United States.

China is still a Communist nation. But its leaders are working to make China a nation with modern farms, factories, and technology. More people own businesses. China trades with the United States and other countries. Nations are building factories in China. China is becoming a modern nation. But people in China still do not have many freedoms.

Today many people in Asia's industrial nations enjoy western activities like movies, baseball, and music. But **traditions** are still important in Asia. Asians still enjoy religions, music, clothing, stories, and dances from long ago. However, people in Asia are looking to the future. They are trying to find ways to make their lives better.

Using Vocabulary

Find the Meaning   Write on the blank the word or words that best complete each sentence.

1. **Poverty** means having very little _____.

   money   time   power

2. **Traditions** are ways of life that people have _____.

   forgotten   followed for many years   changed

3. A leader who has been **assassinated** has been _____.

   elected   punished   killed

4. Countries that have a problem with **illiteracy** have many people who do not

   know how to _____.

   read or write   grow crops   find jobs

5. Nations that are **trading partners** _____ from one another.

   collect taxes   buy goods   refuse to buy products

Read and Remember

Finish Up   Choose a word in dark print to best complete each sentence. Write the word on the correct blank line.

Pakistan   farming   developing   Bangladesh   Asia

1. More than half of the world's population is in _____.

2. Most people in _____ nations do not make as much money as do people in industrial nations.

3. India's Muslims started the nation called _____ in 1947.

4. Only a small part of the land of Japan is used for _____.

5. Terrible floods in _____ in 1988 left millions of people without homes.

Think and Apply

Compare and Contrast   Read each sentence below. Decide whether the sentence tells about India, Japan, or both countries. Write **I** next to each sentence that tells about India. Write **J** next to each sentence that tells about Japan. Write **IJ** next to each sentence that tells about both India and Japan.

_____ **1.** This is a modern industrial nation.

_____ **2.** This nation is very crowded.

_____ **3.** This country is a democracy.

_____ **4.** Much of this country was destroyed during World War II.

_____ **5.** This nation has had many riots between Hindus and Muslims.

_____ **6.** This nation has had recent trade problems with the United States.

Skill Builder

Reading a Political Map   A **political map** shows how areas of land are divided. Some political maps show how a continent is divided by nations. Thin lines are used to show the borders between nations. Different colors are used to show different nations. Sometimes colors are used more than once. Look at the map of Asia on page 113. This map shows how Asia is divided today. Study the map. Then write the answer to each question.

1. What country shares India's northwest border? _____

2. In what ocean are the Philippines and Taiwan? _____

3. What country in Asia is the largest? _____

4. What island nation is east of South Korea? _____

5. What two nations are between Russia and China? _____

_____

6. What is the capital city of India? _____

Journal Writing

Gandhi was a very important leader in India's history. Write a few sentences that tell some of the ways that Gandhi worked to help India.

Skill Builder

Reading a Double Bar Graph
A **double bar graph** compares facts by using two different colored bars. This double bar graph shows how the populations of India and Japan changed from 1980 to 1995. Study the graph. Then write the answer to each question.

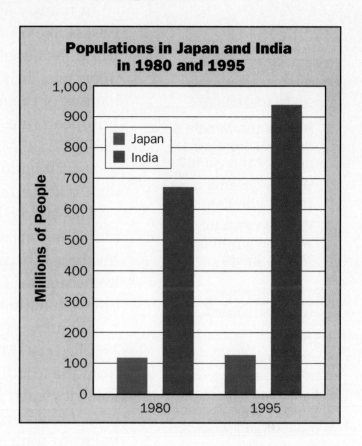

1. What color are the bars that show the population of Japan?_____

2. Which nation has more people?_____

3. Which nation's population only increased a small amount from 1980 to

1995? _____

4. About how many more people lived in India in 1995 than in 1980?_____

_____

5. About how many more people lived in India than in Japan in 1995?

_____

CHAPTER 16

The Middle East Today

THINK ABOUT AS YOU READ

1. How is the Middle East different from other parts of the world?
2. What problems does the Middle East have?
3. Why have so many wars occurred in the Middle East?

NEW WORDS

♦ shah
♦ embassy
♦ hostages
♦ homeland
♦ Six-Day War
♦ Palestine Liberation Organization
♦ terrorists
♦ terrorism

PEOPLE & PLACES

♦ Arab
♦ Iran
♦ Ayatollah Khomeini
♦ Saddam Hussein
♦ Palestinians
♦ Jordan
♦ Syria
♦ Yasir Arafat
♦ Yitzhak Rabin
♦ King Hussein I

In many ways the Middle East is like other areas of the world. Nationalism is very important. It helped many nations of the Middle East become independent from European rule. Religion is also very important in the Middle East. Many countries are trying to become industrial nations. But the Middle East is also very different from other areas of the world.

The Middle East is the only region in which most of the nations are Arab nations. Most Arabs are Muslims. There are also millions of Christian Arabs in the region. The Middle East is the only region with a Jewish nation. This is the small nation of Israel.

About two thirds of the world's oil is found in the Middle East. Many industrial nations buy their oil from the Middle East. They need this oil for their factories, cars, and homes.

There are many problems in the Middle East today. In some nations, poverty and illiteracy are

People from many cultures shop in a market in Jerusalem.

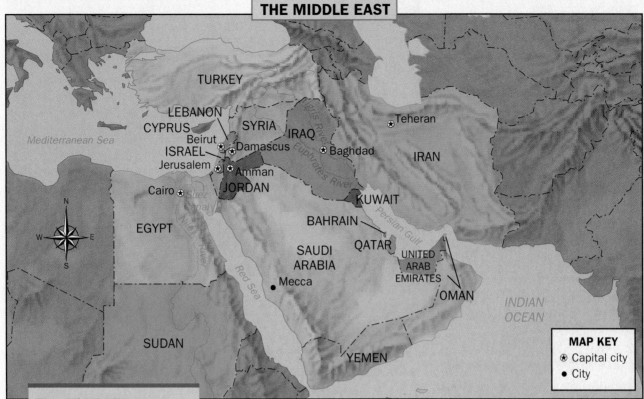

THE MIDDLE EAST

TURKEY

LEBANON
CYPRUS
SYRIA
IRAQ
*Teheran

Mediterranean Sea
Beirut
Damascus
Baghdad
IRAN
ISRAEL
Jerusalem
Amman
JORDAN
KUWAIT

Cairo
BAHRAIN
EGYPT
QATAR
UNITED
ARAB
EMIRATES
SAUDI
ARABIA
•Mecca
OMAN
INDIAN
OCEAN

SUDAN
YEMEN

MAP KEY
⊛ Capital city
• City

The Middle East has
many Arab nations. In
which nation is the city
of Mecca located?

problems. Most nations do not have enough water.
They cannot grow all the food they need. Many
nations have little industry. They do not make many
products to sell to other nations. There are not
enough doctors. A large problem is war. Wars have
occurred all over the Middle East. Many of the wars
have been about religion or the control of oil fields.

In the late 1970s, Muslims in Iran forced the
shah, or king, of Iran to leave the country. The
Ayatollah Khomeini, a Muslim religious leader,
became the nation's leader. A new government was
started that was based on the laws of Islam.
Everyone in Iran had to follow the laws of Islam.
People in Iran were not allowed to use ideas,
clothing, music, or businesses that were from
European nations or the United States.

The shah of Iran had fled to the United States.
People in Iran were angry that the United States
protected the shah. In 1979 a group of people in Iran
attacked the United States **embassy**. They forced the

Ayatollah Khomeini

People from Iraq set hundreds of Kuwait's oil wells on fire during the Persian Gulf War. It was very difficult to stop the fires.

Angry Muslims in Iran burning an American flag

Saddam Hussein

Americans in the embassy to become **hostages**. Iran refused to release the hostages unless the shah was returned to Iran for a trial. The shah died in 1980. Finally in 1981, the Americans were set free.

In 1980 the Arab nation of Iraq attacked Iran. Iraq was led by President Saddam Hussein. About one million people were killed or injured in the war. Finally in 1989 the United Nations helped the two nations agree to a cease-fire.

Iraq needed money after the war with Iran. In 1990 Iraq invaded Kuwait in order to control Kuwait's oil fields. The UN told Iraq to leave Kuwait, but Iraq refused. The United States and other UN countries from Europe and the Middle East sent troops to help free Kuwait. Iraq and the UN signed a cease-fire agreement to end the Persian Gulf War. But since then, Saddam Hussein has broken some of the promises he made in the cease-fire agreement.

Since 1948 four wars have occurred between Arab nations and Israel. Israel was once part of the land of Palestine. Jews had lived there for thousands of years. After World War II, many Jews wanted Palestine to be their **homeland**. In 1947 the UN divided Palestine into two parts. One part would be ruled

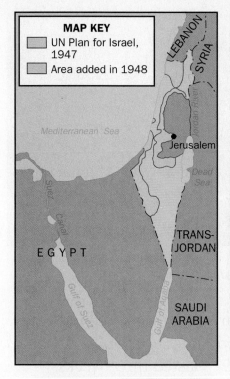

MAP KEY
- UN Plan for Israel, 1947
- Area added in 1948

MAP KEY
- Israel in 1948
- Area held by Israel in 1967

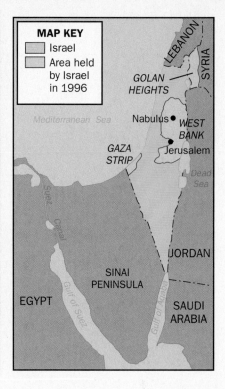

MAP KEY
- Israel
- Area held by Israel in 1996

Israel held other lands after different wars with Arab nations. Compare the first two maps above. Which area of Egypt did Israel hold in 1967?

Israelis fighting in Jerusalem during the Six-Day War

by Arabs who lived there. These Arabs were called Palestinians. The other part would be ruled by Jews. In 1948 the Jewish part became the state of Israel.

Many Arabs did not like the UN plan. They did not want any part of Palestine to be a Jewish nation. In 1948 five Arab countries invaded Israel. The UN helped end the fighting. But Israel controlled more of Palestine than it had before the war of 1948. Many Palestinians fled from Israel. About 700,000 Palestinian refugees went to live in other Arab lands.

There was another war in 1956. This war was between Israel and Egypt. Again the UN helped end the fighting. Israel remained free.

In 1967 the Arabs and the Israelis fought again. After six days the Arabs surrendered. During the **Six-Day War,** Israel captured lands that had been ruled by Egypt, Jordan, and Syria. Israel still controls some of these lands.

In 1973 there was a fourth war against Israel. The war was started by Egypt and Syria. Israel fought back with weapons from other countries. This time the Arabs used their oil as a weapon. They stopped

Thousands of Palestinians live in refugee camps. Many of these refugee camps have become small towns.

selling oil to all the countries that were helping Israel. After that, only the United States and Holland would help Israel. The war in 1973 lasted three weeks. Israel won the war. Israel remained a free nation.

In 1979 Egypt became the first Arab nation to sign a peace treaty with Israel. The United States helped the two nations write the peace treaty. In 1982 Israel returned to Egypt land that had been captured in 1967. Egypt and Israel have kept their promises to live in peace.

For more than forty years, many Palestinians have lived in refugee camps in Arab nations. The United Nations pays for food, medicine, and schools for the camps. The refugees cannot return to Israel. Most refugees have not been allowed to become citizens of other Arab lands.

The **Palestine Liberation Organization** (PLO) was formed in 1964. The goal of the PLO is to have a Palestine nation again. Yasir Arafat is the leader of the PLO. For years the PLO said there should not be a Jewish nation in the Middle East. Many PLO members and other Arabs have become **terrorists**. They have bombed buses, planes, schools, and stores. Terrorists have killed Israelis and other people who have helped Israel. These Palestinians believe that **terrorism** will help them win their own nation.

Yasir Arafat

President Bill Clinton of the United States helped the leaders of Israel and of the PLO reach a peace agreement in 1993.

Yitzhak Rabin

King Hussein I

In 1988 Yasir Arafat said that the PLO would accept Israel as a nation. In 1991 the Israelis and the Palestinians started peace talks. In 1992 the Israelis elected Yitzhak Rabin as prime minister of Israel. Rabin worked to make peace between Israel and its Arab neighbors. In 1993 Israel and the PLO signed a peace agreement. Israel agreed to return some land to the Palestinians. Rabin and Arafat received the Nobel Peace Prize for their work toward peace.

In 1994 Jordan became the second Arab nation to sign a peace treaty with Israel. The United States helped King Hussein I of Jordan and Rabin of Israel write the treaty. Jordan and Israel have agreed to work together to solve problems.

In 1995 Yitzhak Rabin and Yasir Arafat signed another peace agreement. That same year Rabin was assassinated by an Israeli. The man who killed Rabin said that he was protesting the peace agreements between the Arabs and the Israelis.

The Middle East is still troubled by war and terrorism. But nations are trying to find ways to make peace. Perhaps one day lasting peace will come to the people of the Middle East. Then they can work together to solve the problems of the Middle East.

USING WHAT YOU LEARNED

Using Vocabulary

Finish Up   Choose the word in dark print to best complete each sentence. Write the word on the correct blank line.

> **embassy   terrorism   homeland   hostage   shah**

1. The _____ was the king of Iran.

2. In 1947 the United Nations said that part of Palestine should be a Jewish _____, or country.

3. Attacks on people, planes, and schools are examples of _____.

4. A _____ is a person who is being held prisoner.

5. An _____ is the headquarters of a representative from another nation.

Read and Remember

Finish the Paragraph   Use the words in dark print to finish the paragraph below. Write on the correct blank lines the words you choose.

> **Jordan   Iraq   Six-Day War   Arab**
> **war   oil   Yasir Arafat   Muslims**

The Middle East is a region that has many _____ nations. The Middle East is very rich in _____. One of the Middle East's biggest problems is _____. In 1979 _____ in Iran forced the shah to leave the country. _____ invaded Kuwait in 1990. There have been four wars in Israel. One was the _____ in 1967. Since then, the nation has signed peace treaties with Egypt and _____. The prime minister of Israel also worked with _____ for peace between Israel and the PLO.

Think and Apply

Exclusions   One word or phrase in each group does not belong. Find that word or phrase and cross it out. Then write on a separate sheet of paper a sentence that tells how the other words are alike.

1. poverty
illiteracy
not enough water
oil

2. laws of Islam
leader was Khomeini
hostages from embassy
Palestinian refugees

3. leader was Saddam Hussein
ally of the United States
attacked Iran in 1980
started the Persian Gulf War

4. prime minister of Israel
signed treaty with Arafat
member of the PLO
assassinated in 1995

Skill Builder

Reading a Circle Graph   A **circle graph** shows how all of something is divided into parts. Most often a circle graph shows **percent,** or parts per one hundred. This circle graph shows how the world oil supply was divided among regions of the world in 1994. Study the circle graph. Then draw a circle around each correct answer.

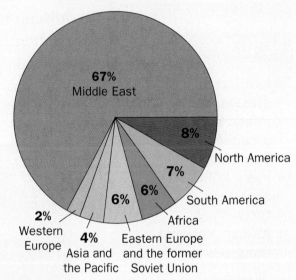

World Oil in 1994

67%
Middle East

8%
North America

7%
South America

6%
Africa

6%
Eastern Europe
and the former
Soviet Union

4%
Asia and
the Pacific

2%
Western
Europe

1. Which region had the largest amount of oil?

Western Europe   Middle East   Africa

2. Which region had the same amount of oil as Eastern Europe and the former Soviet Union had?

Africa   North America   Asia and the Pacific

3. What was the total percent of the world oil in the Americas?

8%   15%   73%

CHAPTER 17

Africa Today

THINK ABOUT AS YOU READ

1. What are some of the problems in Africa today?
2. Where have some civil wars occurred in Africa?
3. How is Africa working to solve its problems?

NEW WORDS

♦ rain forests
♦ grasslands
♦ ethnic groups
♦ droughts
♦ starvation
♦ mass killings
♦ apartheid
♦ tribal chief
♦ African National Congress

PEOPLE & PLACES

♦ Nigeria
♦ Zaire
♦ Rwanda
♦ Hutu
♦ Tutsi
♦ Coloreds
♦ Nelson Mandela

Africa is the world's second largest continent. There are 53 nations in Africa today. Africa has **rain forests,** mountains, and **grasslands**. The Sahara is the world's largest desert. The Nile River is the world's longest river.

Africa is very rich in natural resources. South Africa has most of the world's gold. It also has a lot of the world's diamonds. Nigeria is rich in oil. Zaire is rich in copper and diamonds. Many nations buy natural resources from Africa.

Africa has more than 800 **ethnic groups**. Each group has a different language and culture. Some African nations have hundreds of ethnic groups. It is often hard for the groups to get along. Problems between the ethnic groups have caused civil wars.

Some of the world's earliest civilizations began in Africa. During the 1400s, Europeans began to explore

People in Eritrea celebrated the African nation's independence in 1992.

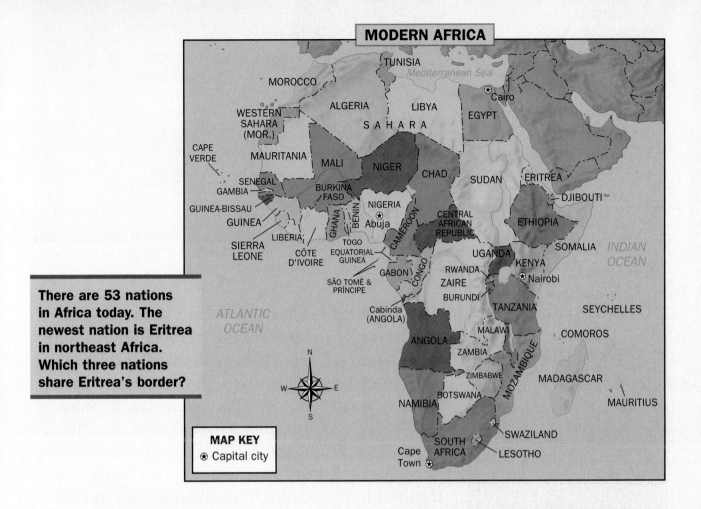

MODERN AFRICA

TUNISIA
MOROCCO
Mediterranean Sea
WESTERN SAHARA (MOR.)
ALGERIA
LIBYA
EGYPT
✪ Cairo
S A H A R A
CAPE VERDE
MAURITANIA
MALI
NIGER
CHAD
SUDAN
ERITREA
SENEGAL
BURKINA FASO
DJIBOUTI
GAMBIA
GUINEA-BISSAU
NIGERIA
✪ Abuja
CENTRAL AFRICAN REPUBLIC
ETHIOPIA
GUINEA
GHANA
BENIN
TOGO
SIERRA LEONE
LIBERIA
CÔTE D'IVOIRE
EQUATORIAL GUINEA
CAMEROON
UGANDA
SOMALIA
INDIAN OCEAN
GABON
CONGO
RWANDA
KENYA
✪ Nairobi
SÃO TOMÉ & PRÍNCIPE
ZAIRE
BURUNDI
ATLANTIC OCEAN
Cabinda (ANGOLA)
TANZANIA
SEYCHELLES
ANGOLA
MALAWI
COMOROS
ZAMBIA
MOZAMBIQUE
MADAGASCAR
ZIMBABWE
NAMIBIA
BOTSWANA
MAURITIUS
SWAZILAND
Cape Town ✪
SOUTH AFRICA
LESOTHO

N W E S

MAP KEY
✪ Capital city

There are 53 nations in Africa today. The newest nation is Eritrea in northeast Africa. Which three nations share Eritrea's border?

Women in a village in the African country of Kenya

Africa. They forced many Africans to work as slaves in Europe and in colonies. Most of the slave trade ended by the early 1800s. After the Industrial Revolution began, Europe wanted raw materials from Africa. Soon most of Africa was ruled by imperialist nations. After World War II, nationalism became important to Africans. From 1950 to 1980, 47 colonies in Africa gained independence.

Many nations of Africa are developing nations. Poverty, hunger, and illiteracy are big problems. The biggest problem is that Africa's population is growing very fast. The nations do not have enough food or schools for the people.

Most people in Africa live in small villages. Most are farmers who work the same way that farmers worked long ago. The soil is often poor. The farmers are not able to grow enough food for everyone.

As the city of Cairo, Egypt, grows, new buildings are sometimes built around ancient statues.

People watching lions in Africa

Oil workers in Nigeria

Droughts have made problems worse for many nations. During a drought there is very little rain for many months. There is not enough water to grow food. During the 1980s and 1990s, there have been terrible droughts in many parts of Africa. Millions of people have died because of droughts. Most of these people starved to death.

Nigeria is a developing nation in western Africa. It gained independence from Great Britain in 1960. Nigeria has the largest population in Africa. More than 100 million people live there.

In the 1970s Nigeria earned a lot of money by selling oil to industrial nations. In the 1980s the price of oil went down. Nigeria could not earn enough money by selling oil. The nation learned that it needs to sell many different kinds of products to other nations.

Nigeria has more than 250 ethnic groups. In 1967 a civil war between ethnic groups began in Nigeria. It ended in 1970. More than two million people died in the war. Since then the people of Nigeria have worked to rebuild their nation.

In 1991 a civil war also broke out in Somalia. The civil war and a drought caused the **starvation** of more than 270,000 Somalians. In 1992 the United Nations sent troops to Somalia to try to bring peace and food to the nation. Many people were saved

More than four million refugees fled Rwanda to escape the mass killings in 1994.

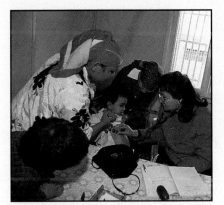
Doctor examining children in Africa

Worker in a South African mine

from starvation, but the UN failed to bring peace to Somalia. The civil war continued. UN troops left Somalia in 1995.

The African country of Rwanda has had civil wars between two main ethnic groups, the Hutu and the Tutsi. In 1994 some of the Hutu tried to kill all of the Tutsi in Rwanda by **mass killings**. More than 750,000 people were killed during the civil war. About four million refugees fled from Rwanda to nearby African countries. But fighting has also occurred in the refugee camps. The UN is trying to help bring food and peace to the camps.

South Africa is the most developed nation in Africa today. It is an industrial nation that is rich in resources. The nation has good soil. Farmers grow most of the food that the nation needs.

Around 1650 many Dutch people moved to South Africa. In 1820 people from Great Britain began to move to South Africa. South Africa was part of the British empire for many years. In 1931 South Africa became an independent nation.

Beginning in the late 1940s, South Africa passed laws called **apartheid**. These laws divided people into four groups. White people belonged to the smallest group. Coloreds belonged to the second

Discrimination in South Africa

The city of Nairobi in Kenya

Children in school in Sierra Leone, Africa

group. Coloreds are people that come from mixed Black, White, and Asian families. Asians were the third group. Black Africans were the fourth and largest group.

The purpose of apartheid was to keep the four groups of people apart. The laws gave Whites full power to rule the nation. Blacks were not allowed to vote. Members of each group were not allowed to marry members of other groups. Blacks and Whites could not use the same hotels, beaches, schools, or hospitals. Blacks were forced to live in the poorest parts of South Africa. They worked at difficult jobs for low wages.

South African Blacks and some South African Whites worked hard to end apartheid. They became protesters. One Black protest leader, Nelson Mandela, was kept in prison for 27 years. He was finally freed in 1990.

People around the world were also angry about the apartheid laws. The UN told South Africa to change its laws. Some nations stopped trading with South Africa. Finally in 1991, South Africa ended most of its apartheid laws. In 1993 South Africans agreed to a new constitution. Blacks were given the right to vote. The country is becoming a democracy. In 1994 Nelson Mandela was elected president of South Africa. Many other Blacks were elected to Parliament. South Africa is trying to find ways for all groups of people to take part in the government.

Nations in Africa are trying to find ways to work together to solve their problems. Africans are using their natural resources to improve their lives. More children are going to school. Nations are trying to become more modern. New factories are being built. Farmers are learning ways to grow more food. Workers from the United Nations are also helping African countries. Perhaps one day there will be less poverty, hunger, and civil war in Africa. Perhaps one day there will be more peace and unity.

Nelson Mandela (1918–   )

Nelson Mandela was born in South Africa in 1918. His father was a **tribal chief** of an ethnic group in South Africa. Nelson Mandela was trained to be a tribal chief. But he chose to go to college to become a lawyer.

In 1944 Mandela joined the **African National Congress** (ANC). The ANC was the largest Black group against the South African government. During the 1950s Mandela became famous for leading protests against the South African government. His role in these protests finally led to his arrest in 1956. Mandela was found not guilty and was released.

In 1960 the South African government said it was against the law to belong to the ANC. This did not stop Mandela. He led more protests against the South African government. In 1962 Mandela was arrested again. This time he was found guilty. He was sent to prison for life.

Many people began to think of Mandela as a symbol of the protest against apartheid. People in South Africa and around the world called for his release. More protests were held in South Africa. Finally in 1989, the president of South Africa met with Mandela. Mandela agreed to help work for peace in South Africa. The South African government agreed to allow people to be members of the ANC. Mandela was released from prison in 1990.

Nelson Mandela worked with the South African government to write a new constitution. In 1994 Blacks and Whites voted in the nation's first free election. Mandela was elected president of South Africa. He was the nation's first Black president. Nelson Mandela helped South Africa end apartheid and move toward democracy.

Nelson Mandela

Nelson Mandela voting for the first time in South Africa

Using Vocabulary

Analogies   Use the words in dark print to best complete the sentences.

drought   grasslands   apartheid   starvation

1. Forests are to woods as meadows are to _____ .

2. Tall is to short as flood is to _____ .

3. Bacteria are to diseases as scarce food is to _____ .

4. Caste system is to India as _____ is to South Africa.

Read and Remember

Write the Answer   Write one or more sentences to answer each question.

1. What are four problems found in Africa today? _____

_____

_____

2. What are three African nations in which civil wars have occurred? _____

_____

3. What did the Hutu try to do in Rwanda in 1994? _____

_____

4. What was the purpose of apartheid in South Africa? _____

_____

Journal Writing

Nelson Mandela was a symbol of the protest against apartheid in South Africa. Write a paragraph that tells what Mandela did to bring change to South Africa.

Skill Builder

Reading a Population Map
A **population map** shows the number of people living in different places. The map key of a population map gives colors or patterns to show different numbers of people. This map shows about how many people per square mile live in Africa. Study the map and the map key. Then draw a circle around each correct answer.

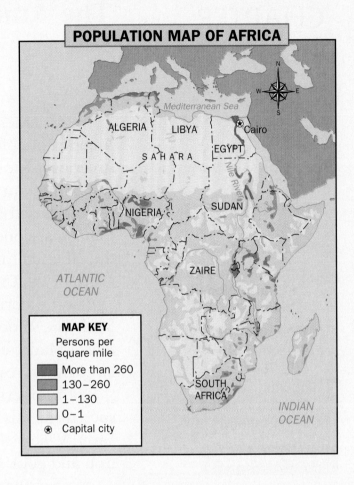

POPULATION MAP OF AFRICA

MAP KEY
Persons per square mile
More than 260
130–260
1–130
0–1
⊛ Capital city

1. How many people per square mile does most of the nation of South Africa have?

   0–1   1–130   more than 260

2. Which of these countries has the fewest people per square mile?

   Libya   Zaire   South Africa

3. Which of these three nations has the most people per square mile?

   Nigeria   Algeria   Sudan

4. What part of Egypt has the highest population?

   along the border of Libya   along the border of Sudan

   along the Nile River

5. Where do most people in Africa live?

   south of the Sahara   in Cairo   in the Sahara

CHAPTER 18

The Americas Today

North America and South America are often called the Americas. The Americas sometimes are divided into two regions based on culture. The United States and Canada are one **cultural** region. Latin America is the other cultural region. All of the countries to the south of the United States are part of Latin America.

Latin American countries have many types of land. The Andes Mountains and the mountains of the Sierra Madre cover thousands of miles. There are large rain forests, deserts, grasslands, and beaches.

Latin America also has many natural resources, such as metals and trees. Mexico is rich in oil and silver. Venezuela is also rich in oil. Brazil is rich in iron and gold. Chile is rich in copper.

Most of the people of Latin America speak Spanish. Portuguese is the language of Brazil. Some people speak American Indian languages. Most people are Roman Catholics.

THINK ABOUT AS YOU READ

1. **What are the two cultural regions in the Americas?**
2. **What are some of the problems in Latin America?**
3. **In what ways are Canada and the United States alike?**

NEW WORDS

♦ cultural
♦ gap
♦ inflation
♦ debt
♦ repay
♦ extinct
♦ North American Free Trade Agreement
♦ illegal drugs

PEOPLE & PLACES

♦ Sierra Madre
♦ Portuguese
♦ Fidel Castro
♦ Rocky Mountains
♦ Great Plains
♦ Great Lakes

The beautiful Andes Mountains are some of the tallest mountains in the world.

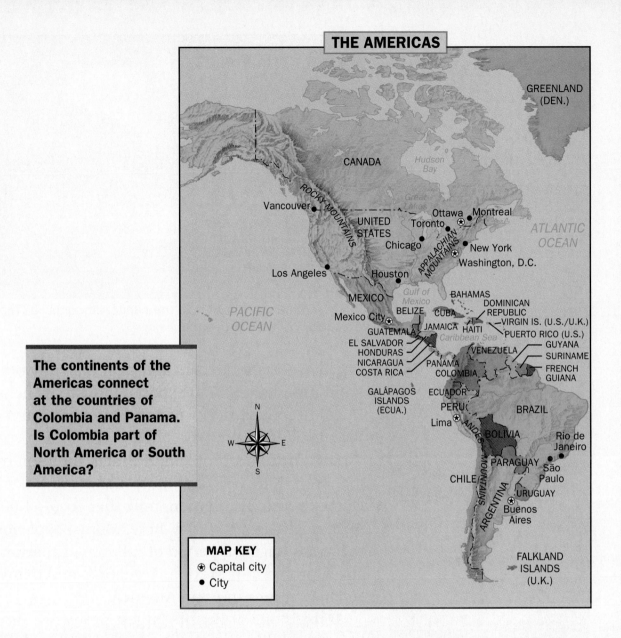

THE AMERICAS

GREENLAND (DEN.)

CANADA

Hudson Bay

ROCKY MOUNTAINS

Vancouver

UNITED STATES

Ottawa   Montreal
Toronto
Chicago

Great Lakes

APPALACHIAN MOUNTAINS

New York
Washington, D.C.

ATLANTIC OCEAN

Los Angeles   Houston

PACIFIC OCEAN

MEXICO

Gulf of Mexico

BAHAMAS

Mexico City   BELIZE   CUBA
GUATEMALA   JAMAICA   HAITI

DOMINICAN REPUBLIC
VIRGIN IS. (U.S./U.K.)
PUERTO RICO (U.S.)

Caribbean Sea

EL SALVADOR
HONDURAS
NICARAGUA
COSTA RICA

PANAMA
COLOMBIA

VENEZUELA

GUYANA
SURINAME
FRENCH GUIANA

GALÁPAGOS ISLANDS (ECUA.)

ECUADOR
PERU
Lima

ANDES MOUNTAINS

BRAZIL

BOLIVIA

Rio de Janeiro

PARAGUAY

São Paulo

CHILE

ARGENTINA

URUGUAY
Buenos Aires

FALKLAND ISLANDS (U.K.)

N
W   E
S

MAP KEY
⊛ Capital city
● City

The continents of the Americas connect at the countries of Colombia and Panama. Is Colombia part of North America or South America?

People walking on a beach in Puerto Rico

In Latin America today, there is a very big **gap** between the rich and the poor. Most people are very poor. Not many people are part of the middle class. Rich people are part of a small, powerful group. They own most of the land and the factories. They have the most power in the government. Latin American nations are trying to end this gap. Some governments are giving land to the poor. In some nations the middle class is growing larger.

Brazil is the largest nation in Latin America. It is becoming a developed nation. For many years, Brazil earned most of its money by exporting coffee. Today,

The government of Brazil is in the capital city Brasília. The city is known for its many modern buildings.

Ships carrying goods from Brazil

Poverty in Brazil

Brazil exports more cars and steel than any other Latin American nation exports. Industry is helping Brazil become a richer nation. But many parts of Brazil still have poverty.

Inflation is a problem in Brazil. Inflation means that everything becomes more and more expensive. During a year of inflation, milk that costs $1.00 in April might cost $3.00 by June. Many people lose their jobs during a period of inflation. Inflation is also a problem in Mexico, Argentina, and many smaller nations in Latin America.

Debt is one of Brazil's largest problems. Brazil borrowed billions of dollars from the United States, Japan, and other nations. The Portuguese used the money to build roads, schools, and factories. Brazil must **repay,** or pay back, this money. Brazil now uses most of its money to repay its debt.

Brazil has the world's largest rain forest. Much of the rain forest is destroyed each year. Trees are cut down and cleared away. The land is then used for farming or for roads. Many important resources in rain forests are lost when the trees are destroyed. Some plants and animals have become **extinct**.

Mexico is a democracy. Like Brazil, Mexico is becoming a developed nation. Mexican factories

People have been destroying the rain forests in Brazil in order to create new farmland.

Air pollution in Mexico City

A border crossing between Mexico and the United States

export cars, steel, and clothing to other nations. Mexico also exports oil, coffee, and sugar.

Mexico is working to solve many problems. Its cities have terrible pollution from cars and factories. Poverty is another problem. Like Brazil, Mexico also has inflation and a very large debt.

In the 1970s Mexico earned a lot of money by selling oil to other nations. In the 1980s the price of oil went down. Mexico was forced to sell its oil for less money. It had to borrow billions of dollars. Now Mexico must repay its debt. Many people have lost their jobs. Many Mexicans have become poorer. Some of these Mexicans have tried to move to the United States.

The government of Mexico is working hard to make Mexico a better place to live. It has built many schools in all parts of Mexico. Today, most Mexicans know how to read and write. The government has given farmland to many poor people. The middle class is growing larger.

Cuba is a Communist nation. For many years Cuba has worked to spread communism to other Latin American countries. Fidel Castro is the leader of Cuba. He is a dictator. He has been in power since 1959. Since then, hundreds of thousands of Cuban

Fidel Castro

A Cuban immigrant in the United States

The White House, home of the President of the United States

immigrants have moved to the United States. These people did not want to live in a Communist country. They did not like the way Castro ruled Cuba.

Many nations in Latin America are struggling with revolutions and unfair governments. Some nations have been ruled by many different dictators. But people are working to bring peace to Latin America. Many people are working to give everyone in Latin America a good life. New industries are being started. The nations of Latin America are exporting more products. Cities are growing larger. Many schools are built each year.

Like many Latin American nations, the United States and Canada have many types of land. The Rocky Mountains, the Great Plains, and the Great Lakes are found in both nations. Both countries are rich in natural resources. They have fertile soil, forests, coal, iron ore, and oil.

The United States and Canada are alike in many ways. They are both world powers and democracies. They are industrial nations with high standards of living. The United States and Canada also have some of the same problems. Some of their natural resources, such as trees and fish, are being used up. Pollution from factories and cars is another problem.

The United States, Canada, and Mexico are major trading partners. In 1993 the three nations passed the **North American Free Trade Agreement** (NAFTA). NAFTA will help trade among the three countries increase.

The United States is one of the world's strongest nations. It creates new technology and medicines. It works hard to help many nations end hunger, civil war, and poverty. It helps many nations fight the spread of communism and the rise of dictators. It also works for stronger world trade. People from many different nations have moved to the United States. The United States has been called "a nation of immigrants."

More than 150,000 people gathered in Montreal, Quebec, about whether Quebec should leave the nation of Canada.

Fireworks above the Statue of Liberty in New York City

Rodeo in Alberta, Canada

The United States is working to end problems with Latin America. One way it does this is through trade. It is also trying to end the movement of **illegal drugs** from some Latin American countries into the United States. Illegal drugs are dangerous drugs that are against the law to sell and to use in a nation.

Canada is the second largest country in the world. It was once part of the British empire. The two main languages in Canada are English and French. Like the United States, Canada works to bring peace and to end problems in other nations.

Many Canadians who speak French live in the area of Quebec. Many of the people in Quebec feel that Quebec should be its own nation. But in 1995 the people of Quebec voted to remain part of the nation of Canada.

The nations of the Americas help one another in many ways. They are increasing trade with one another and are working to end poverty and pollution. Each year the nations of the Americas are finding more ways to work together.

Using Vocabulary

Finish the Paragraph Use the words in dark print to finish the paragraph below. Write on the correct blank lines the words you choose.

gap   repay   inflation   debt   extinct

There are many problems in Latin America today. Pollution is a problem.

There is a large _____, or amount of differences, between the

rich and the poor. Many goods in Latin America are becoming more expensive.

This is called _____. Some Latin American countries borrowed

millions of dollars that they must _____, or pay back. When a

nation owes money, the nation has a _____. Whole groups of

animals and plants in the rain forests of Brazil are dying, or becoming

_____.

Read and Remember

Choose the Answer Draw a circle around the correct answer.

1. How are the Americas often divided into regions?

based on population   based on culture   based on natural resources

2. Which nation exports more cars and steel than any other Latin American nation exports?

Brazil   Mexico   Cuba

3. Which is the smallest class of people in Latin America?

the rich   the middle class   the poor

4. Which three nations signed NAFTA?

Brazil, Argentina, and Canada   Mexico, the United States, and Canada

Cuba, Canada, and Great Britain

Finish the Sentence   Draw a circle around the word or words that best complete each sentence.

1. Portuguese is the language of _____.

Mexico   Cuba   Brazil

2. Mexico had to borrow money after the price of _____ went down in the 1980s.

oil   farmland   diamonds

3. Fidel Castro became the leader of _____ in 1959.

Argentina   Chile   Cuba

4. Mexico has terrible pollution from _____.

cars and factories   rain forests   debt

5. One problem between the United States and some Latin American nations is _____.

hunger   illegal drugs   standard of living

Think and Apply

Distinguishing Relevant Information   Imagine that you want to tell a friend about the ways that the United States and Canada are alike. Read each sentence below. Decide which sentences are relevant to what you will say. Put a check (✔) next to the relevant sentences. There are four relevant sentences.

_____ **1.** Both nations are industrial nations and democracies.

_____ **2.** The Rocky Mountains and the Great Plains can be found in both nations.

_____ **3.** Trees, fish, and other natural resources are being used up.

_____ **4.** The people of Quebec voted to remain part of Canada.

_____ **5.** There is a large gap between the rich and the poor.

_____ **6.** The nations work to spread peace and to prevent the rise of dictators in other nations.

Skill Builder

Reading a Double Line Graph   A **double line graph** compares facts by using two different lines. The lines on this graph show how the populations of the Americas have changed over time. On this graph, North America includes the United States and Canada. Latin America includes Mexico. Study the graph. Then write the answer to each question.

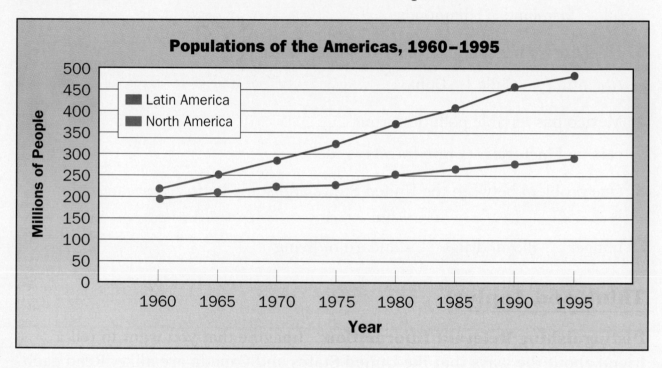

Populations of the Americas, 1960–1995

1. What color is used to show the population of North America? _____

2. About how many people were living in North America in 1980? _____

3. About how many more people were living in Latin America in 1995 than in

   1965? _____

4. About how many more people were living in Latin America than in North

   America in 1995? _____

5. In what year were the populations of Latin America and North America

   about the same? _____

6. Which region's population increased the most? _____

144

CHAPTER 19

Europe Today

Europe is a continent with many nations, languages, and cultures. Its land has many hills, mountains, peninsulas, and plains. There are many canals, ports, and harbors

that help Europeans trade with nations around the world. Some nations of Europe are rich in natural resources, such as iron, coal, and oil. Today most of Europe has many kinds of industries. Factories produce cars, chemicals, steel, and other items.

After World War II, Europe became divided into two regions—Eastern Europe and Western Europe. During the Cold War, the people in the Communist countries of Eastern Europe had a lower standard of living than did the people of Western Europe. Many goods were scarce. Most people were not able to own cars or washing machines.

THINK ABOUT AS YOU READ

1. Why did communism grow weaker in Eastern Europe?
2. How did communism end in nations such as Poland and the Soviet Union?
3. How does the EU work to help the nations of Europe?

NEW WORDS

♦ Solidarity
♦ freedom of the press
♦ Channel Tunnel
♦ European Union
♦ Common Market
♦ shipyards
♦ trade unions
♦ candidates

PEOPLE & PLACES

♦ Polish
♦ Lech Walesa
♦ Mikhail Gorbachev
♦ Yugoslavia
♦ Gdansk

Many people enjoy visiting the beautiful city of Prague, the capital of the Czech Republic.

Europe is a continent with many peninsulas. Which of these three countries is on a peninsula: Ireland, Romania, or Italy?

Mikhail Gorbachev

The people in Eastern Europe and in the Soviet Union grew tired of communism. People wanted more freedom and a better standard of living. During the 1980s the governments of Eastern Europe and the Soviet Union began to change. These changes gave people more freedom. People began to demand the end of communism.

Poland was the first nation in Eastern Europe in which communism grew weaker. In 1980 Polish workers started a labor union called **Solidarity**. Solidarity worked to create a non-Communist government. In 1989 Poland had its first free election since the Cold War began. Lech Walesa, the leader of Solidarity, became the president of Poland.

Communism grew weaker in the Soviet Union soon after Mikhail Gorbachev became the nation's leader in 1985. He allowed people to have freedom of speech and **freedom of the press**. There was also more religious freedom. People began to own farms, factories, and businesses.

Thousands of people gathered to watch the Berlin Wall being torn down by the East Germans in 1989.

By 1991 communism in the Soviet Union had grown very weak. The nation began to fall apart. It was divided into 15 republics. Russia was the largest of these republics. Russia and other republics held free elections. Communism ended. The once strong Soviet Union was no longer a nation.

Throughout Eastern Europe, people voted in free elections for new leaders. Communism in Eastern Europe ended. This brought an end to the Cold War.

The people of East Germany and West Germany had wanted the two nations to become united again. In 1989 many people gathered to watch as the Berlin Wall was torn down. East Berlin and West Berlin became one city again. In 1990 East Germany and West Germany united. Today Germany is a non-Communist nation.

Modern factory in Germany

In 1991 and 1992, changes also occurred in the Communist nation of Yugoslavia. During this time, Yugoslavia was divided into six different republics. Four republics declared their independence. One of these nations was Bosnia and Herzegovina.

In the year 1992, a civil war began in Bosnia and Herzegovina. The war began because three ethnic groups fought to win control of the new country.

Many buildings were destroyed during Bosnia's civil war. This man is taking bricks from a library in order to rebuild his home.

Train going into the Channel Tunnel

A market in Spain

Much of Bosnia was destroyed. The UN and NATO sent troops to the nation to help stop the fighting there. In 1995 the United States helped the leaders of the ethnic groups agree to a peace plan. But there is still tension between the groups.

The nations of Europe are working to improve relations with one another. One way that Great Britain and France did this was to make it easier to travel between the two nations. They built a tunnel for trains under the English Channel. The **Channel Tunnel** opened in 1994.

Fifteen nations of Western Europe are members of the **European Union** (EU). This organization makes it easier for member nations to sell goods and services to one another. The EU makes it easier for people of one nation to work in another EU nation. The EU helps to lower the prices of many goods and services in Europe. The EU was called the European **Common Market** when it first began. Many nations in Eastern Europe hope to one day join the EU.

The European Union is working to make Europe a more united continent. By 1999 the EU plans to have one money system for all member nations. As European nations work for better business and trade, they will also be working for peace.

Lech Walesa (1943–   )

Poland became a Communist nation in 1945. By the 1980s communism was growing weaker in Poland. Workers were going on strike. Their leader was Lech Walesa. He became a symbol of freedom in Eastern Europe. Walesa and the workers helped end communism in Poland.

Lech Walesa was born in Poland during World War II. In 1967 he began working in the **shipyards** in Poland's port city Gdansk. He joined the strikes for workers' rights. In 1980 Walesa became the leader of Solidarity. Solidarity was a non-Communist organization of **trade unions**. The members of Solidarity held protests and went on strike. They wanted lower food prices and better wages.

Lech Walesa

In 1981 the Communist government arrested Walesa and some other members of Solidarity. In 1982 government leaders said that it was against the law for people to be members of Solidarity. Walesa was released from prison in 1982. In 1983 Walesa received the Nobel Peace Prize for using peaceful ways to gain workers' rights.

In 1989 Poland's government allowed people to join Solidarity. Changes were made in Poland's government. Non-Communists were allowed to be **candidates** in elections. Free elections were held. In 1990 Walesa became president of Poland. Poland became a non-Communist nation.

Lech Walesa speaking during a workers' strike in Poland

Poland was one of the first Eastern European nations to end its Communist government. However, Poland faced new problems. Prices for many goods increased. Many people did not have jobs. Workers went on strike. In 1995 Walesa lost the election for president. But Lech Walesa is respected for working to end communism in Poland.

Using Vocabulary

Find the Meaning   Write on the blank the word or words that best complete each sentence.

1. The **Channel Tunnel** is an underwater railway tunnel between

_____ and France.

Great Britain   Germany   the United States

2. The **European Union** is an organization that makes it easier for member

countries to _____.

fight communism   hold free elections   sell goods and services

3. The **Common Market** is another term for _____.

NAFTA   the UN   the EU

4. **Solidarity** was a non-Communist organization of _____ in Poland.

candidates   trade unions   government leaders

Read and Remember

Find the Answer   Put a check (✔) next to each sentence that tells about Europe today. You should check four sentences.

_____ **1.** The nations of Europe are working together to improve trade and relations with one another.

_____ **2.** The Soviet Union spread communism to Eastern Europe.

_____ **3.** Europe has many natural resources and many different industries.

_____ **4.** A Communist government owns most farms and businesses.

_____ **5.** The EU is trying to make Europe a more united continent.

_____ **6.** It is becoming easier for people in one European nation to work in another European nation.

Finish the Paragraph   Use the words in dark print to finish the paragraph below. Write on the correct blanks the words you choose.

Poland   **communism**   **Cold War**   **West Germany**
standard   **Berlin Wall**   **republics**

The people of Eastern Europe had a lower _____ of living

than did the people of Western Europe. During the 1980s the people of Eastern

Europe demanded the end of _____ . In 1989 the people

of _____ held free elections. During that same year the

_____ was torn down. In 1990 East Germany and

_____ were united as one nation. In 1991 the Soviet Union

was divided into 15 separate _____ . The end of communism

brought an end to the _____ .

Think and Apply

Fact or Opinion   Write **F** next to each fact below. Write **O** next to each opinion. You should find three opinions.

_____ **1.** Many goods were scarce in Eastern Europe.

_____ **2.** Communism should end in Eastern Europe.

_____ **3.** Mikhail Gorbachev was the best ruler of the Soviet Union.

_____ **4.** The European Union plans to have one money system for all member nations.

_____ **5.** The Common Market is a good way to improve trade between the nations of Europe.

_____ **6.** The civil war in Bosnia and Herzegovina began in 1992.

_____ **7.** Lech Walesa and Solidarity helped bring an end to communism in Poland.

Unit 5   Looking to the Future

The world continues to change all the time. Nations are learning new ways to work together. They are increasing trade and improving relations. People are living longer. Populations are growing. New inventions are being made. They are quickly changing the way we live. Many inventions make life better. People are finding new ways to travel and to share information.

As we look toward the year 2000 and beyond, we can see many challenges facing the world. Nations know that they need one another to get the things they do not have. They want to have good relations with other nations. They want to work together to make the world better. Nations are working together to end poverty and hunger and to protect the earth. They are finding ways to keep world peace and to protect freedom. People are working together to solve pollution and health problems.

It is hard to know for sure what the future will be like. However, it is important to solve the problems we have today in order to have a better tomorrow. It is also important to learn from past mistakes, such as the reasons that wars have been fought. If we learn from our mistakes, we can prevent the same problems from happening again.

ATLANTIC OCEAN

PACIFIC OCEAN

PACIFIC OCEAN

INDIAN OCEAN

How can we stop pollution? How can nations be better neighbors? What can we do now to make sure we have a better future? As you read Unit 5, think about how the world is changing. Think about what you can do to build a better world for tomorrow.

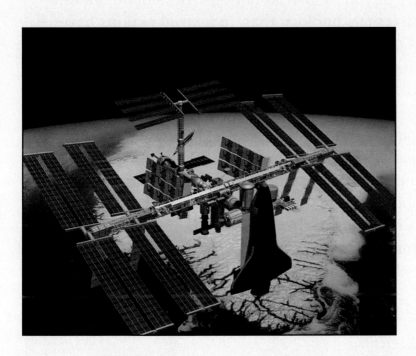

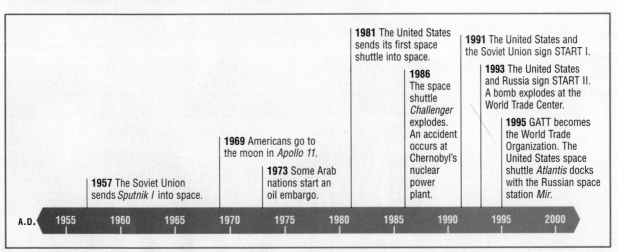

1957 The Soviet Union sends *Sputnik I* into space.

1969 Americans go to the moon in *Apollo 11*.

1973 Some Arab nations start an oil embargo.

1981 The United States sends its first space shuttle into space.

1986 The space shuttle *Challenger* explodes. An accident occurs at Chernobyl's nuclear power plant.

1991 The United States and the Soviet Union sign START I.

1993 The United States and Russia sign START II. A bomb explodes at the World Trade Center.

1995 GATT becomes the World Trade Organization. The United States space shuttle *Atlantis* docks with the Russian space station *Mir*.

A.D.   1955   1960   1965   1970   1975   1980   1985   1990   1995   2000

Technology Brings Change

Technology has changed the world in many ways since World War II. It has changed the ways people travel, work, and share information. It has helped doctors save lives and businesses grow. There is new technology being used every day in industrial nations. Developing nations have less technology than industrial nations have.

Computers have become very important in many nations. Before the 1970s few people had computers in their homes or schools. Industrial nations now have computers everywhere. Computers are used in airplanes and spaceships. They are in banks, offices, schools, stores, and homes. Every year people make computers that can do more things. Computers have become smaller, cheaper, and more useful.

Communication is better than ever before. Communication is how people share information. People **communicate** with one another by talking,

THINK ABOUT AS YOU READ

1. How has technology changed the ways we live?
2. How has technology improved space travel?
3. How have computers and satellites helped communication?

NEW WORDS

- communication
- communicate
- cellular phones
- fax machines
- Internet
- electronic mail
- fertilizers
- bullet trains
- astronauts
- space shuttles
- space station
- orbit
- docked

Computers have become an important part of schools and businesses.

Today farmers are learning ways to grow food using little soil and water.

Person using a cellular phone on a beach in Thailand

Computers are used in many offices.

writing, or touching. People can communicate using telephones, televisions, radios, and computers. Today people can use **cellular phones** to call people from cars or while outdoors. People can also use **fax machines** to send copies of papers and pictures to one another over telephone lines.

Computer owners can also use the **Internet** to share information. The Internet is a large system of computers all over the world that are linked to one another. Messages can be sent very quickly by **electronic mail** from one computer user to another user on the Internet. Electronic mail is sometimes called e-mail. People can also use the Internet to look up information about many subjects.

Technology is part of the agricultural revolution. You have read how new farming machines were invented during the Industrial Revolution. At that time a farmer who worked hard could grow enough food for four people.

Technology has helped farmers grow much more food. Large farm machines can do the work of many farmers. Farmers now use **fertilizers** that help the soil produce more food. Farmers are able to irrigate farms that are far from lakes and rivers. In some

The bullet train in Japan can travel over 150 miles an hour.

Modern wheat farming

places farmers have turned deserts into fertile farm land. Farmers can grow much more food from new kinds of wheat and rice seeds. One farmer today can grow enough food for more than eighty people.

Technology has changed the way we travel. Long ago explorers had to sail for many days in order to cross an ocean. Today a person can fly out of Great Britain after breakfast and eat dinner in New York City. Airplanes have made it easier for people to travel around the world.

On land, trains are an important way to travel. **Bullet trains** in some nations can travel faster than 150 miles per hour. France has trains that travel faster than 185 miles per hour. Modern technology has also made it possible to build underwater tunnels like the Channel Tunnel between Great Britain and France. These tunnels allow trains to travel between lands that are separated by miles of water.

Technology has helped people travel into space. Space travel began in 1957 when the Soviet Union sent the first satellite into space. The first Soviet satellite was called *Sputnik I*. Less than one year later, the United States sent its first satellite into space. The space race became part of the Cold War. Both nations began sending people into space. People who travel in space are called **astronauts**. As time passed, astronauts took longer trips into space.

The United States is a leader in space technology. The space shuttle can travel into space many times.

Communications satellite

In 1969 Americans became the first people to walk on the moon. The Americans went to the moon in a spaceship called *Apollo 11*. It took only four days to fly to the moon.

For many years, spaceships could be used for only one trip into space. The United States began building spaceships that could be used many times. These new spaceships were called **space shuttles**. In 1981 Americans took their first trip in a space shuttle. Since then the United States has built other space shuttles.

Space travel has not always been safe. In 1986 a space shuttle called *Challenger* exploded soon after it went into the sky. All seven people on board the space shuttle were killed. After that, Americans worked to build safer shuttles. In 1988 they began to send shuttles into space again.

In 1986 the Soviets put a new **space station** into **orbit** around Earth. The station is called *Mir*. People can stay in the space station for many months. The station helps us learn more about space and Earth.

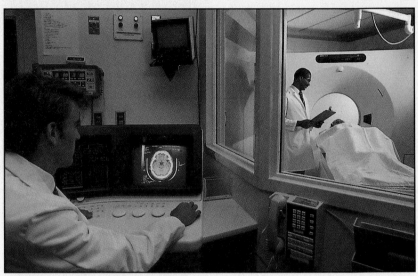
Technology has greatly improved medicine. New machines help doctors save many lives.

A satellite dish receives information from satellites.

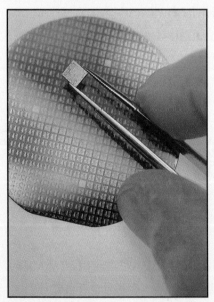
Computers use tiny computer chips to run.

In 1995 and 1996, the United States space shuttle *Atlantis* **docked** with the *Mir* space station. The Russians and the Americans worked together on experiments in space.

Today the United States and Russia are still leaders in space technology. Japan, France, China, Canada, and other nations have their own space programs. Many nations have sent satellites into space. Nations are trying to learn more about Earth and other planets. Several nations are working together to build a new space station.

Space satellites have helped communication. There are hundreds of space satellites in the sky for communication. Weather satellites help us learn when dangerous storms are coming. Some satellites help us make telephone calls to faraway nations. Television satellites help us watch shows from many nations of the world. Satellites can also send news reports from one nation to another as events occur.

Technology has helped nations learn more about one another. It has also helped the growth of trade. Technology has made nations need one another in many ways. Why do nations need one another? How do nations work together to solve problems? You will find the answers in the next chapter.

Using Vocabulary

Finish Up   Choose the word or words in dark print to best complete each sentence. Write the word or words on the correct blank line.

orbit   communication   bullet   electronic mail   Internet

1. The act of sharing information with other people is called

_____ .

2. The _____ is a system of computers that are linked to one another.

3. Computer owners can send messages to other computer owners using a

system called _____ .

4. Trains that can travel over a hundred miles an hour are sometimes called

_____ trains.

5. To be in _____ is to travel around a planet.

Read and Remember

Finish the Sentence   Draw a sentence around the word or words that best complete the sentence.

1. Developing nations have less _____ than industrial nations.

natural resources   people   technology

2. People can use _____ phones to call people while in a car or outdoors.

orbit   cellular   e-mail

3. Astronauts are people who travel in _____ .

bullet trains   space   fax machines

4. Weather _____ let us know when dangerous storms are coming.

fertilizers   shuttles   satellites

Think and Apply

Exclusions   One word or phrase in each group does not belong. Find that word or phrase and cross it out. Then write on a separate piece of paper a sentence that tells how the other words are alike.

1. *Sputnik I*
   Apollo 11
   Atlantis
   Challenger

2. fertilizers
   new kinds of seeds
   satellite
   large farm machines

3. satellites
   e-mail
   space station
   space shuttles

4. cellular phones
   Internet
   astronaut
   fax machines

Sequencing Events   Write the numbers **1, 2, 3, 4,** and **5** next to these sentences to show the correct order.

_____ The United States space shuttle *Atlantis* docked with the *Mir* space station in 1995 and 1996.

_____ Space travel began when the Soviet Union sent its first satellite into space.

_____ In 1969 American astronauts reached the moon after traveling in a spaceship for four days.

_____ The seven people on board the *Challenger* died when the space shuttle exploded in 1986.

_____ United States astronauts traveled in the first space shuttle, a spaceship that could be used many times.

Journal Writing

Technology has changed the world in many ways. Write a paragraph that tells three ways that technology has helped people. Give examples from the chapter.

Nations Depend on One Another

THINK ABOUT AS YOU READ

1. Why do nations need one another?

2. Why is trade important today?

3. What are some problems that many nations face?

NEW WORDS

♦ interdependence
♦ scarcity
♦ interdependent
♦ General Agreement on Tariffs and Trade
♦ tariffs
♦ World Trade Organization
♦ natural gas
♦ gasoline
♦ import
♦ oil embargo
♦ nuclear power plants
♦ radioactive wastes
♦ acid rain

PEOPLE & PLACES

♦ Chernobyl
♦ Ukraine

Nations work together for many reasons. Together they trade, work for world peace, and solve problems such as hunger and pollution. **Interdependence** brings nations closer together. Interdependence means that nations need one another for many things. It also means that the problems of one nation can hurt other nations.

Scarcity makes nations need one another. Scarcity means that many people and businesses do not have enough of the products or raw materials that they need. There is a scarcity of oil and coal in many nations. There is a scarcity of food and technology in many developing nations. Nations need one another to get the things they do not have.

Nations became **interdependent** long ago when they began trading with one another. The ancient Romans got silk and foods from far-off lands. About the year 1500, Europeans conquered many lands in

Nations depend on one another for trade. This large tanker is carrying oil from one nation to another.

Ships carry goods all over the world. These goods are being shipped from Bombay, India's largest port.

Worker in a car factory in Mexico

order to gain colonies. They wanted silks, spices, gold, and silver from their colonies. After the Industrial Revolution, nations got raw materials such as cotton and coal from their colonies.

Trade is very important in the modern world. Trade helps nations get the goods and the raw materials they need. Japan has become one of the world's richest nations because of trade. Japan has few natural resources. It buys raw materials from other nations. Japan uses these raw materials to make factory products. Every year, Japan exports goods that earn billions of dollars.

In 1947 many countries worked together to set up the **General Agreement on Tariffs and Trade** (GATT). This organization helped increase trade between member countries by lowering **tariffs**. Tariffs are special taxes on traded goods. Tariffs make goods more expensive. In 1995 GATT became the **World Trade Organization** (WTO).

As you read in Chapter 18, the United States, Canada, and Mexico agreed to NAFTA. This trade agreement was created to help trade between the three nations. NAFTA helps trade by lowering or removing tariffs. NAFTA also makes it easier for the

President Clinton of the United States signed NAFTA in 1993.

Oil wells are used to get oil from beneath land and oceans.

Electric power lines

people in each nation to own businesses or to work in the other two nations.

All industrial nations need energy for their offices, factories, homes, and cars. Light, heat, and electricity are three kinds of energy. Most nations use oil, coal, and **natural gas** to make energy. In many places most energy is made from oil. **Gasoline** is made from oil. Most cars and trucks use oil and gasoline. Oil is used to make electricity. There is a scarcity of oil in many industrial nations. They must **import** oil from the nations of the Middle East, Africa, and Latin America.

During the Arab-Israeli war of 1973, it was hard for many nations to get the oil they needed. This is because the Arabs started an **oil embargo**. They stopped selling oil to the United States and to some other nations. The oil embargo made it hard for people to buy gasoline for cars. Electricity became more expensive. Many people wanted to find new ways to make energy without using oil.

Some countries began to make electricity in **nuclear power plants**. These plants used nuclear energy instead of oil to make electricity. There are many nuclear power plants in Europe and the United

Nuclear power plants provide a way to make electricity without using coal, oil, or natural gas.

Nuclear power plant in Chernobyl

Traffic is one cause of air pollution.

States. A nuclear power plant can be very dangerous if there is an accident in the plant.

In 1986 a terrible accident happened at a nuclear power plant in the Soviet Union. The plant was located in the city of Chernobyl. Today Chernobyl is part of the nation Ukraine. The accident at the plant sent a lot of **radioactive wastes** into the air. Winds blew these radioactive wastes over other nations in northern Europe. Many people died right after the accident. Many animals died from the radioactive wastes. Doctors believe that many people who live near Chernobyl will continue to get cancer from the spread of radioactive wastes.

Each year industrial nations have more cars and factories. These cars and factories cause air pollution and water pollution. Pollution makes air and water unsafe. Sometimes air pollution in one nation becomes part of the rain. Then the rain becomes **acid rain**. Acid rain sometimes falls on other nations. These nations might be far from where the pollution first began. Acid rain kills plants and animals. Acid rain is damaging rivers, lakes, and forests in Europe and in North America.

The world's rain forests are being destroyed. These rain forests have many natural resources. You have

Many buildings and statues become damaged from air pollution. Here a man cleans a damaged statue in Venice.

Trees damaged by acid rain

Tree frogs and many other animals live in rain forests.

read about the rain forests in Brazil. Rain forests can also be found in Asia, Africa, and other parts of Latin America. People chop down the trees in rain forests to use the land for farms and cities. Some people export wood and other resources from these forests. About half of the world's rain forests have been destroyed.

What happens when trees are destroyed by people or by acid rain? Trees help clean Earth's air. Without trees, air and water become more polluted. Trees hold fertile soil to the earth. Without trees, fertile soil is washed away. Thousands of plants and animals live only in rain forests. When rain forests are destroyed, the plants and animals are also destroyed. The rain forests are important to all the people of the world. Nations must work together to save these forests.

There is great interdependence between nations today. Nations are working together to solve trade and energy problems. They are learning ways to protect Earth's land, air, and water. Nations are working together to make the world better.

Using Vocabulary

Match Up   Finish the sentences in Group A with words from Group B. Write the letter of each correct answer on the blank line.

Group A

1. When nations need one another for many things, it is called _____.

2. There is a _____ of food when a nation does not have enough food to feed its people.

3. Special taxes that make traded goods more expensive are _____.

4. When rain has been affected by air pollution, it is called _____ rain.

Group B

a. tariffs

b. acid

c. interdependence

d. scarcity

Read and Remember

Finish the Paragraph   Use the words in dark print to finish the paragraph below. Write on the correct blank lines the words you choose.

**animals   nuclear power   interdependent
radioactive   rain forests**

Nations are _____, because the problems of one nation can hurt other nations in the world. In 1986 a terrible accident happened at a _____ plant in the Soviet Union. The accident sent lots of _____ wastes into the air. The wind blew this pollution over other nations in northern Europe. In Asia, Africa, and Latin America, _____ are being destroyed. When these places are destroyed, the plants and _____ that live there are also destroyed.

Finish Up   Choose the word or words in dark print to best complete each sentence. Write the word or words on the correct blank line.

cancer   GATT   trees
import   gasoline   nuclear power

1. _____ was an organization that helped increase trade by lowering tariffs.

2. Oil is used to make electricity and _____.

3. Some nations use _____ plants to make electricity without using oil.

4. Doctors believe that people who live near Chernobyl will continue to get

_____.

5. Without _____, air and water become more polluted.

6. Nations must _____ goods from other nations.

Think and Apply

Categories   Read the words in each group. Decide how they are alike. Find the best title for each group from the words in dark print. Write the title on the line above each group.

Pollution   Oil Embargo
Kinds of Energy   Used to Make Energy

1. _____   3. _____
   light   wastes in the water
   electricity   wastes in the air
   heat   acid rain

2. _____   4. _____
   electricity became expensive   oil
   Arab-Israeli war   coal
   gasoline was hard to buy   natural gas

CHAPTER 22

Working for Tomorrow

THINK ABOUT AS YOU READ

1. **How can nations solve the problem of nuclear weapons?**
2. **What are some new ways to make energy?**
3. **How can nations protect Earth's land, air, and water?**

NEW WORDS

♦ **START I**
♦ **START II**
♦ **conserve**
♦ **solar energy**
♦ **oil spills**
♦ **fumes**
♦ **AIDS**
♦ **virus**
♦ **HIV**
♦ **World Health Organization**
♦ **house arrest**

PEOPLE & PLACES

♦ **Mexico City**
♦ **Los Angeles**
♦ **George Bush**
♦ **Boris Yeltsin**
♦ **Scotland**
♦ **Aung San Suu Kyi**
♦ **Myanmar**

As years pass, the world changes in many ways. Today, people of all nations have many new problems to solve. We must work for tomorrow by solving today's problems.

Nuclear weapons are a problem that nations must solve. The United States dropped the first atomic bombs on Japan during World War II. For many years, the United States and the Soviet Union had a nuclear arms race. China, France, Great Britain, and India also have made atomic bombs. Some of today's bombs are much more powerful than those used in World War II.

Many people are afraid that there might be a nuclear war some day. If one nation uses its nuclear weapons, then other nations might fight back and use their own nuclear weapons. Atomic bombs

The United States and Russia are destroying many of the airplanes that are used to carry nuclear weapons.

might destroy much of the earth. One powerful atomic bomb could kill millions of people. For this reason, some nations are trying to make sure that nuclear weapons are never used again.

In 1991 President George Bush of the United States and President Mikhail Gorbachev of the Soviet Union signed a treaty called **START I**. Both nations promised to destroy many dangerous weapons and to make fewer nuclear weapons. That same year the Soviet Union divided into 15 republics. President George Bush worked on another treaty with Russia's president, Boris Yeltsin. In 1993 Bush and Yeltsin signed a treaty called **START II**. In this treaty both nations agreed to destroy even more nuclear weapons.

George Bush and Boris Yeltsin signing START II

You have learned that industrial nations use coal, oil, and natural gas to make energy. Many people believe that one day the earth's supplies of coal, oil, and natural gas will be used up. The nations of the world now have two big energy problems. One problem is to find different ways to make energy. The other problem is to learn how to **conserve,** or save, energy for tomorrow.

Scientists are finding new ways to make energy. Some people are using energy from the sun. This is called **solar energy**. Solar energy can heat homes. It can heat water for homes and factories. Water power from many rivers is used to make electricity. Wind can also be used to make electricity. Many nations use nuclear energy to make electricity.

People can now use wind to create electricity.

People in industrial nations are learning ways to conserve energy. People save energy by using less electricity. They turn off lights that are not being used. They use less heat in the winter. They wash clothes in cold water. People try to use their cars less often. They save energy by riding on buses and trains instead of driving their cars.

Pollution has become a serious problem in every industrial nation. Air pollution from cars and

A terrorist bomb destroyed an airplane over Scotland in 1988. All 147 people on board were killed.

People cleaning up a major oil spill in Alaska in 1989

Nations are starting to make cars that run on electricity.

factories has become a big problem in cities such as Mexico City and Los Angeles. It is not healthy to breathe the air in those cities. Water pollution has killed fish and plants in many lakes in the United States and in other nations. **Oil spills** from ships have caused serious water pollution in many oceans and seas. Acid rain is damaging forests and lakes in Canada and in Europe. There are problems like these in many nations of the world.

Some nations are trying to protect Earth's land, air, and water. These nations have laws that prevent factories from dumping garbage into oceans, lakes, and rivers. Other laws force factories to send less pollution into the air. Cars are being built that send fewer **fumes** into the air. Some cars use electricity instead of oil. Nations are also working on ways to prevent oil spills from ships. Oil spills in oceans can kill many fish, birds, and other animals.

Terrorism is a problem for many countries today. In 1988 a terrorist bomb caused a large American airplane to explode over Scotland. All 147 people on the plane were killed. In 1993 a terrorist bomb exploded at the World Trade Center in New York

By helping solve the problem of pollution, people are working for a better tomorrow.

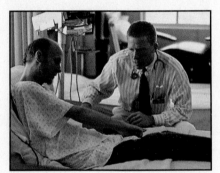
Doctor examining a person who has AIDS

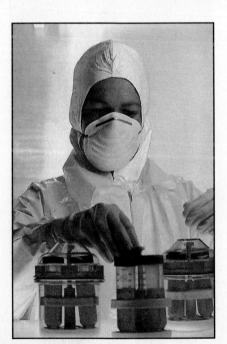
People are working to find a cure for AIDS.

City. Terrorism has occurred in many nations, including France, Great Britain, Israel, and Japan. Many governments are working together to try to end terrorism.

Today the world faces a new problem—the disease called **AIDS**. This disease is caused by a **virus** called **HIV**. AIDS kills more and more people each year. There is no cure for AIDS at this time. Doctors in many nations are studying the disease in order to find a cure. The **World Health Organization** is also working to find a cure for AIDS. The World Health Organization is a part of the United Nations.

In many nations today, people enjoy freedom. They enjoy equal rights with all the people of their nations. But in many parts of the world, people are not free. In some nations, such as China and Iraq, people are killed for speaking against their government. The leaders of free nations are working for freedom all over the world.

In the years ahead, people will continue to work for a better tomorrow. You will also have a chance to work for a better future. You will vote for future government leaders. You might work with scientists and leaders to solve many important world problems. In those ways, you will be writing the next chapter in *World History and You.*

Aung San Suu Kyi (1945–   )

Aung San Suu Kyi is the leader of the fight for democracy in Myanmar. Myanmar is a developing nation in Southeast Asia. Before 1989 Myanmar was called Burma. It has a military government. The people of Myanmar have few rights and little freedom. Since 1988 Aung San has been working to bring democracy to Myanmar. In 1991 she won the Nobel Peace Prize for her peaceful efforts to change Myanmar's government.

Aung San Suu Kyi

Aung San Suu Kyi was born in Rangoon, Burma, in 1945. Her father, Thakin Aung San, led the nation's fight for independence from Great Britain. Burma won its independence in 1948. Since 1962 the nation has had a military government. In 1988 Aung San Suu Kyi helped form the National League for Democracy (NLD), the main group against the military government. In 1989 Aung San was put under **house arrest** for her role in the NLD. She was not put in prison, but she also was not allowed to leave her home.

In 1990 the government allowed NLD candidates to be in an election for Myanmar's parliament. Aung San's group won most of the votes. But the government would not allow the new parliament to meet. Some representatives were sent to prison.

Aung San was held under house arrest for six years. During that time she wrote a book called *Freedom from Fear and Other Writings*. In 1995 Aung San was released by the government. Since her release, she has given many speeches to encourage democracy and human rights in Myanmar. The government has arrested hundreds of people who support Aung San. But Aung San Suu Kyi continues the struggle for change in Myanmar.

Aung San giving a speech from her home

Using Vocabulary

Find the Meaning Write on the blank the word or words that best complete each sentence.

1. **START I** was a treaty signed by the United States and the Soviet Union to

   destroy many _____ .

   dangerous weapons   rain forests   cities

2. To **conserve** is to _____ .

   buy   save   use up

3. **Solar** energy is energy that comes from _____ .

   oil   wind   the sun

4. **AIDS** is a terrible _____ that has killed many people.

   bomb   oil spill   disease

5. A person who is under **house arrest** is not allowed to _____ .

   stay home   leave home   watch television

Read and Remember

Find the Answer Put a check (✔) next to each sentence that tells something true about the ways nations work for a better tomorrow. You should check four sentences.

_____ **1.** Some nations are making fewer nuclear weapons.

_____ **2.** Scientists are finding ways to use the wind and the sun to make energy.

_____ **3.** People use their cars more often.

_____ **4.** Nations build more factories that cause air pollution and acid rain.

_____ **5.** Some nations have laws to protect the air and water.

_____ **6.** The leaders of free nations work for freedom all over the world.

Glossary

acid rain   page 164
Acid rain forms when pollution in the air becomes part of the rain.

African National Congress   page 133
The African National Congress is a group that works for the rights of South African blacks.

AIDS   page 171
AIDS is a disease in which the body cannot fight germs. AIDS kills more people each year.

alliances   page 43
Alliances are agreements between nations to work together in order to do something.

apartheid   page 131
Apartheid was a system of laws that kept groups of people apart in South Africa.

arrested   page 56
A person who has been arrested has been held by police.

assassinated   page 114
A person who has been assassinated has been killed for a particular reason.

astronauts   page 156
People who travel in space are astronauts.

atomic bomb   page 79
An atomic bomb is a very powerful weapon.

Axis Powers   page 65
The Axis Powers were a group of nations that fought the Allies during World War II.

bacteria   page 13
Bacteria are tiny living things. Some bacteria cause diseases.

Battle of Britain   page 71
The Battle of Britain was a German attack on Great Britain during World War II.

Battle of Stalingrad   page 72
The Battle of Stalingrad was a battle during World War II between Germans and Soviets.

better relations   page 99
Nations that have better relations have found ways to get along with one another.

boat people   page 107
Boat people were refugees who left Southeast Asia by boat during the Vietnam War.

bombed   page 71
A person has bombed something if he or she has caused a bomb to explode.

bombs   page 71
Bombs are weapons that destroy things when they are made to explode.

bullet trains   page 156
Bullet trains are trains that can travel at speeds greater than 150 miles per hour.

canals   page 12
Canals are water routes that cross land to connect rivers, lakes, and oceans.

candidates   page 149
Candidates are people who hope to be elected to a particular office or position.

cease-fire   page 106
A cease-fire is when nations agree to stop fighting.

cellular phones   page 155
Cellular phones are phones that people can use while in a car or outdoors.

Central Powers   page 44
The Central Powers were a group of nations that fought the Allies during World War I.

Channel Tunnel   page 148
The Channel Tunnel is a railway tunnel under the English Channel.

civilians   page 106
Civilians are people who are not in an army or a navy.

civil war   page 55
During a civil war, people of the same nation fight against one another.

Cold War   page 90
The Cold War was a struggle between the United States, the Soviet Union, and other nations about the spread of communism.

collective farms   page 56
Collective farms are farms that are run by groups of people.

Common Market   page 148
The Common Market was the first name of the European Union.

communicate   page 154
To communicate is to share information.

communication   page 154
Communication is how people share information.

communism   page 53
Communism is a system in which most farms and factories are owned by the government.

Communist   page 53
A Communist nation is a nation that uses communism as the system of government.

concentration camps   page 63
Concentration camps were prisons where captured people were sent by Nazis during World War II. Millions of Jews and other people were killed in the camps.

conflict   page 90
A conflict is a war or fight about something.

conserve   page 169
To conserve is to save or keep for later use.

cotton gin   page 7
A cotton gin is a machine that pulls the seeds from cotton. It was invented in 1793.

cotton mills   page 21
Cotton mills are factories that prepare cotton for making thread and cloth.

cultural   page 136
Cultural means having to do with the way of life of a group of people.

Cultural Revolution   page 101
The Cultural Revolution was a time of change in China to make communism stronger.

czars   page 52
Czars were rulers of Russia from the 1500s to the early 1900s.

damage   page 107
Damage is harm that makes something less useful.

D-Day   page 77
D-Day was June 6, 1944. On this date the Allies landed on the beaches of Normandy.

debt   page 138
Debt is money that is owed.

declared war   page 29
If a nation says that it is going to fight in a war against another nation, it has declared war on that nation.

delegates   page 86
Delegates are people who are chosen to represent a group or a nation.

developed nations   page 113
Developed nations are nations that have modern industries and technology, as well as high standards of living.

developing nations   page 112
Developing nations are nations with low standards of living, little industry, and a scarcity of many things.

discrimination   page 36
Discrimination is when people are treated differently because of who they are or where they are from.

docked   page 158
A space shuttle has docked with a space station if it has connected to the station.

droughts   page 130
Droughts are long periods of time when there is little or no rain.

electronic mail   page 155
Electronic mail is a way that computer owners can send messages to other computer owners on the Internet.

elements   page 15
Elements are things in nature from which all other materials are made.

embassy   page 121
An embassy is the headquarters of a representative from another country.

ethnic groups   page 128
Ethnic groups are groups of people who have the same language and culture.

European Union   page 148
The European Union (EU) is an organization of nations in Europe that works to improve trade between member nations.

expand   page 35
To expand means to make larger.

export   page 113
To export means to send products from one country to another country.

extinct   page 138
Animals that are extinct will never exist again. Dinosaurs are extinct.

factories   page 5
Factories are places where goods are made.

fax machines   page 155
Fax machines are machines that people use to send or receive copies of pictures or papers over telephone lines.

fertilizers   page 155
Fertilizers are materials added to soil to help the soil produce more food.

Fourteen Points   page 46
The Fourteen Points was a peace plan written by Woodrow Wilson. It was used for the peace treaty after World War I.

freedom of the press   page 146
Freedom of the press is the right to print anything in newspapers and magazines.

fumes   page 170
Fumes are gases that are harmful to breathe.

gap   page 137
A gap between the rich and the poor means that there is a large difference in the amount of money and land owned by these groups.

gasoline   page 163
Gasoline is a liquid made from oil. It can be burned to make energy to power cars.

General Agreement on Tariffs and Trade   page 162
GATT was a group of nations that worked to increase trade between member nations by lowering taxes on traded goods.

General Assembly   page 86
The General Assembly is the part of the United Nations in which each member nation has a vote.

German Confederation   page 30
The German Confederation was a group of 39 German states that were joined together by the Congress of Vienna.

grasslands   page 128
Grasslands are lands that are covered mainly with grass and have few trees.

Great Depression   page 62
The Great Depression was a period of time in which business became very slow. The depression lasted from 1929 to World War II.

Green Revolution   page 113
The Green Revolution is a way of farming that uses more irrigation, more energy, and better seeds to grow more crops.

HIV   page 171
HIV is the virus that causes AIDS.

Holocaust   page 78
The Holocaust was the killing of millions of Jews and other people by the Nazis during World War II.

homeland   page 122
A homeland is a country where a person was born or has a home.

hostages   page 122
Hostages are people who are held by others until certain demands are met.

house arrest   page 172
House arrest is when police force a person to stay in his or her home.

illegal drugs   page 141
Illegal drugs are drugs that are against the law to sell and to use in a country.

illiteracy   page 112
Illiteracy is when people are not able to read or write.

immigrants   page 20
Immigrants are people who move to other countries.

imperialism   page 34
Imperialism is the idea that one nation should rule colonies or other nations.

imperialist   page 34
A nation that controls colonies or other nations is an imperialist nation.

import   page 163
To import means to bring goods into one country from another country.

Industrial Revolution page 4
The Industrial Revolution was a change from making goods by hand to making goods by machine. It began in the 1700s.

industry page 6
An industry is a kind of business in which many people and machines work together.

inflation page 138
Inflation is a rise in the prices of goods and services.

interdependence page 161
Interdependence means that nations need one another for many things.

interdependent page 161
Nations are interdependent when they need one another for many things.

Internet page 155
The Internet is a large system of computers all over the world.

isolationism page 80
Isolationism is when a nation chooses to not become involved in other nations' problems.

kaiser page 31
A kaiser was a German emperor.

Korean War page 92
The Korean War was a war in the 1950s in which North Korea invaded South Korea to make Korea a united Communist nation.

labor unions page 22
Labor unions are groups of workers who work together to solve problems.

League of Nations page 46
The League of Nations was a group of nations that worked for peace after World War I.

Marshall Plan page 91
The Marshall Plan was the United States plan to help rebuild Western Europe after World War II.

mass killings page 131
Mass killings are when many people are killed by other people at one time.

military page 43
Military is anything having to do with the army, navy, soldiers, or weapons of a nation.

missiles page 91
Missiles are rockets. Some missiles carry bombs.

nationalism page 28
Nationalism is feelings of love and pride for one's nation.

natural gas page 163
Natural gas is a gas that is found in the earth. It can be burned to make power.

naval base page 73
A naval base is a place near the sea where a navy keeps ships, weapons, and airplanes.

neutral page 44
A nation that is neutral does not want to fight in a war.

North American Free Trade Agreement page 140
NAFTA is a plan to help improve trade between the United States, Mexico, and Canada.

North Atlantic Treaty Organization page 91
NATO is a military organization of nations that agree to help protect one another from the spread of communism.

nuclear arms race page 91
During the nuclear arms race, the United States and the Soviet Union increased their supplies of powerful weapons.

nuclear power plants page 163
Nuclear power plants are places that use nuclear energy to make electricity.

nuclear war page 93
A nuclear war is a war that is fought with powerful nuclear weapons.

oil embargo page 163
An oil embargo is when nations that produce oil stop selling it to nations that need it.

oil spills page 170
Oil spills happen when ships or factories leak oil into bodies of water.

opium page 37
Opium is a drug that is made from a plant called the opium poppy.

Opium War   page 37
The Opium War was a war fought between China and Great Britain in 1839 about the opium trade.

orbit   page 157
To be in orbit is to travel around a planet. Satellites orbit around Earth.

organization   page 85
An organization is a group of people or nations that agree to work together.

Palestine Liberation Organization page 124
The Palestine Liberation Organization (PLO) is a group of Arabs whose goal is to have a Palestinian nation again.

permanent   page 86
A permanent member of the UN Security Council can never be removed from the council.

Persian Gulf War   page 87
The Persian Gulf War was a war in 1991 fought by UN nations against Iraq in order to free Kuwait.

poison gas   page 45
Poison gas is something that can kill a person who breathes it. Germans used poison gas to kill enemy soldiers during World War I.

poverty   page 112
Poverty is a lack of money, food, and clothing.

power loom   page 7
A power loom is a machine that uses water power to weave thread into cloth.

prime minister   page 28
A prime minister is the leader of the government in some countries.

protested   page 106
To have protested means that a person has marched, given speeches, or done something else in order to show that he or she is against something.

protesters   page 100
Protesters are people who march, give speeches, or do other things in order to show they are against something.

radiation   page 15
Radiation is a type of energy that travels as waves or as very tiny materials. Light, heat, sound, and x-rays are forms of radiation.

radioactive wastes   page 164
Radioactive wastes are dangerous materials that are left over after nuclear energy is produced.

rain forests   page 128
Rain forests are forests with many trees and plants that receive a large amount of rain.

reaper   page 8
A reaper is a machine that cuts wheat quickly.

rebuild   page 80
To rebuild means to build something again.

recover   page 101
To recover means to get better.

refugees   page 107
Refugees are people who leave their country in order to escape danger.

repay   page 138
To repay means to pay back money that is owed.

resist   page 91
To resist means to keep from giving into something.

resolutions   page 86
Resolutions are things that are decided upon by people or nations.

Russian Revolution   page 54
The Russian Revolution was the war fought in 1917 by the Russian people in order to change Russia's government.

satellite   page 91
A satellite is a machine that travels around Earth.

scarcity   page 161
Scarcity is when many people or businesses do not have enough of the products or raw materials that they need.

secretary-general   page 86
The leader of the United Nations is called the secretary-general.

Security Council page 86
The most powerful part of the United Nations is the Security Council. The council can send soldiers to where there is fighting.

seed drill page 5
A seed drill is a machine that pushes seeds into soil to help more plants grow.

sepoys page 36
Sepoys were people in India who were paid by Europeans to be soldiers.

serfs page 52
Serfs were peasants who were not allowed to leave land on which they lived and worked.

shah page 121
The shah was the ruler of Iran.

shipyards page 149
Shipyards are places where ships are built or repaired.

Six-Day War page 123
The Six-Day War was a war fought between the Arabs and the Israelis in 1967.

smallpox page 13
Smallpox is a deadly disease that causes a high fever and many bumps on the skin.

solar energy page 169
Solar energy is energy from the sun.

Solidarity page 146
Solidarity is the name of the first labor union in Poland.

space race page 91
The space race was a struggle in which the United States and the Soviet Union each tried to be the first nation to have new space technology.

space shuttles page 157
Space shuttles are spaceships that can be used many times.

space station page 157
A space station is a place in space where people can live and work for a long time.

Spanish-American War page 37
The Spanish-American War was a war fought in 1898. The United States fought in this war to help Cuba become free from Spain.

spinning jenny page 6
A spinning jenny is a simple machine that can make up to eight threads at one time. A person turns the jenny's wheel.

spinning mule page 7
A spinning mule is a machine that uses water power to spin thread. It can make thread more quickly than a spinning jenny can.

spinning wheels page 6
Spinning wheels are simple machines that are used for making thread. The wheels can be turned by hand or by using a foot pedal.

standard of living page 14
Standard of living is how well a person is able to buy things that he or she needs or wants.

START I and START II page 169
START I was a treaty signed in 1991 by the Soviet Union and the United States. START II was a treaty signed in 1993 by Russia and the United States. In both treaties, the nations agreed to destroy many nuclear weapons.

starvation page 130
Starvation is when a person suffers or dies from a lack of food.

steamboat page 12
A steamboat is a boat that uses a steam engine in order to move.

steam engine page 8
A steam engine is an engine that is run by steam power.

steam locomotive page 11
A steam locomotive is a train car with a steam engine. It pulls other train cars.

strike page 22
A strike is when union members stop working until business owners agree to make changes.

submarines page 45
Submarines are ships that can travel underwater.

surrendered page 46
An army or a nation has surrendered if it has given up in a battle.

tariffs page 162
Tariffs are special taxes on traded goods.

technology page 43
Technology is the inventions that use science to improve the way things are done.

tension page 43
Tension is a harmful feeling of pressure that causes nations to not trust one another.

terrorism page 124
Terrorism is actions against a group of people or a government in order to cause fear and to gain demands.

terrorists page 124
Terrorists are people who kill other people or destroy things in order to cause fear and to gain demands.

trade unions page 149
Trade unions are organizations of workers who work to improve job conditions.

trading partners page 116
Trading partners are nations that buy products from one another.

traditions page 116
Traditions are customs or beliefs that are passed down from parents to their children.

Treaty of Versailles page 46
The Treaty of Versailles was the World War I peace treaty between the Allies and Germany.

trenches page 45
Trenches are long ditches from which soldiers sometimes fight during a war.

tribal chief page 133
A tribal chief is the leader of a group of people who share a language and culture.

troops page 106
Troops are groups of soldiers.

unification page 30
Unification is when states or nations are brought together or joined to become one.

unified page 30
States or nations have become unified if they have been brought together or joined.

United Nations page 85
The United Nations (UN) is a group of nations that work together for peace and to solve world problems.

vaccine page 13
A vaccine is a type of medicine that prevents people from getting a certain disease.

vetoes page 86
A person vetoes a resolution or a law when he or she says no to keep it from being passed.

Vietnam War page 104
The Vietnam War was a war fought between 1957 and 1975 in Southeast Asia about the spread of communism.

virus page 171
A virus is a very tiny thing that causes disease.

wages page 21
Wages are the pay that workers receive.

warlords page 97
Warlords are leaders who use force to rule an area of a country.

Warsaw Pact page 91
The Warsaw Pact was a treaty signed in 1955 by the Soviet Union and other Eastern European nations.

working class page 14
The working class is a large group of people who work with their hands or with machines.

working conditions page 21
Working conditions describe what a person's job is like. Working conditions include the amount of pay, the number of hours worked each day, and the safety of the work place.

World Health Organization page 171
The World Health Organization is part of the United Nations. This organization helps nations build better health systems.

World Trade Organization page 162
The World Trade Organization (WTO) is a group of nations that work together to increase trade between member nations.

World War I page 42
World War I was a war fought by many nations between 1914 and 1918.

World War II page 70
World War II was a major war fought between 1939 and 1945. Nations all over the world became involved in the war.

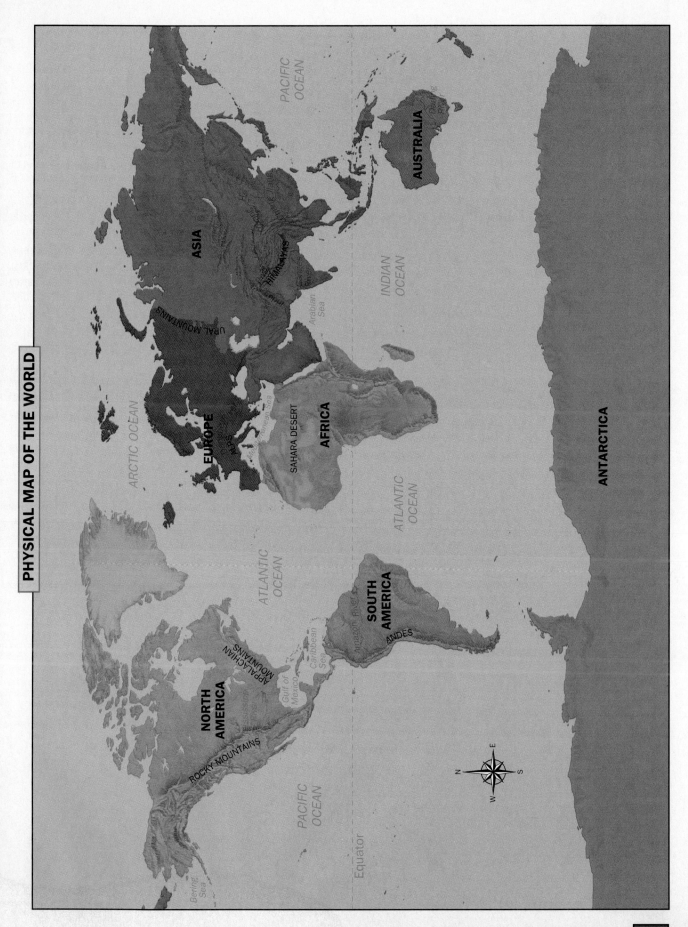

PHYSICAL MAP OF THE WORLD

ASIA

AUSTRALIA

PACIFIC OCEAN

HIMALAYAS

URAL MOUNTAINS

INDIAN OCEAN

Arabian Sea

EUROPE

ALPS

Mediterranean Sea

SAHARA DESERT

AFRICA

ARCTIC OCEAN

ATLANTIC OCEAN

ANTARCTICA

ATLANTIC OCEAN

SOUTH AMERICA

ANDES

Amazon River

Caribbean Sea

APPALACHIAN MOUNTAINS

Gulf of Mexico

NORTH AMERICA

ROCKY MOUNTAINS

PACIFIC OCEAN

Bering Sea

Equator

N

E

W

S

Time Line

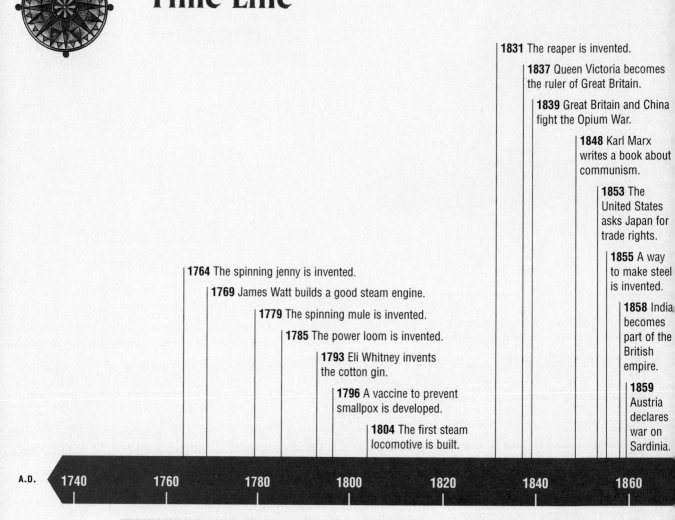

1831 The reaper is invented.

1837 Queen Victoria becomes the ruler of Great Britain.

1839 Great Britain and China fight the Opium War.

1848 Karl Marx writes a book about communism.

1853 The United States asks Japan for trade rights.

1855 A way to make steel is invented.

1858 India becomes part of the British empire.

1859 Austria declares war on Sardinia.

1764 The spinning jenny is invented.

1769 James Watt builds a good steam engine.

1779 The spinning mule is invented.

1785 The power loom is invented.

1793 Eli Whitney invents the cotton gin.

1796 A vaccine to prevent smallpox is developed.

1804 The first steam locomotive is built.

A.D. 1740 1760 1780 1800 1820 1840 1860

1750–1870 Industrial Revolution

1933 Adolf Hitler becomes the dictator of Germany.

1939 Germany invades Poland.

1941 Japan attacks Pearl Harbor.

1945 World War II ends. The United Nations is formed.

1949 China becomes a Communist nation. NATO is formed.

1955 The Warsaw Pact begins.

1957 The Soviet Union sends *Sputnik I* into space.

1961 The Berlin Wall is built.

1967 Arab nations and Israel fight the Six-Day War.

1969 Americans go to the moon in *Apollo 11.*

1980 Iraq attacks Iran.

1991 The Cold War ends. Most apartheid ends in South Africa.

1994 Jordan and Israel sign a treaty.

1995 GATT becomes the World Trade Organization.

1879 Thomas Edison invents the electric light bulb.

1894 Nicholas II becomes Russia's czar.

1898 The Spanish-American war is fought.

1911 Sun Yat-sen helps China become a republic.

1914 World War I begins.

1917 The Russian Revolution occurs.

1920 The League of Nations begins.

| 1880 | 1900 | 1920 | 1940 | 1960 | 1980 | 2000 |

1870–1914 Growth of Imperialism

1929–about 1940 Great Depression

1939–1945 World War II

1945–1991 Cold War

1957–1975 Vietnam War

Index